INDIA
The Roots of Crisis

INDIA
The Roots of Crisis

Satish Saberwal

DELHI
OXFORD UNIVERSITY PRESS
BOMBAY CALCUTTA MADRAS
1986

Oxford University Press, Walton Street, Oxford OX2 6DP

LONDON   GLASGOW   NEW YORK   TORONTO
DELHI   BOMBAY   CALCUTTA   MADRAS   KARACHI
KUALA LUMPUR   SINGAPORE   HONG KONG   TOKYO
NAIROBI   DAR ES SALAAM   CAPE TOWN
MELBOURNE   AUCKLAND
and associates in
BEIRUT   BERLIN   IBADAN   MEXICO CITY

Printed in India
by Urvashi Press, 49/3 Vaidwara, Meerut 250002
and published by R. Dayal, Oxford University Press
YMCA Library Building, Jai Singh Road,
New Delhi 110001

In memoriam
Victor Turner
1920–1983

This work draws on studies during sabbatical leave from
Jawaharlal Nehru University (1980) and during a fellowship at
Nehru Memorial Museum and Library, New Delhi (1982–4)

CONTENTS

PREFACE

This short work concerns the social crisis in India: a situation of widespread uncertainty over the 'rules of the game', of absence of firm, dependable norms expressed in others' and in one's own conduct; a situation of anomie. The air is inevitably thick with consequent anxieties and with varied explanations of every passing event: upheavals in Punjab or in the North-east; the lesser sway of everyday violence in Bihar, Uttar Pradesh, and elsewhere; continual eruptions of communal conflict in one locality after another; growing arbitrariness even in such institutions as the courts and universities . . . the list can go on. Everyday explanations commonly consist of finding scapegoats: one identifies a culprit whose misdeeds are seen to account for what is happening. The scapegoats vary greatly in shape and size, including such entities as 'colonialism', 'the foreign hand', 'Mrs Gandhi's machinations', and 'my difficult X neighbour' where X may stand for Madrasi or Muslim or Jat, or whatever.

How far such an explanation is valid for the matter at issue will vary with the case. The essays in this work meet these phenomena at a different level. I am interested, rather, in the questions of why we in India should have allowed ourselves to be colonized in the first place; why 'the foreign hand' should be able to move so easily among us; why many who control public power can act so short-sightedly and so self-servingly without being called to account; why so many of us should be saddled with, or should believe that we are saddled with, difficult neighbours; and so forth. My interest is in the structures—of institutions, of relationships, of ideas—in which these phenomena arise; and I see these structures as expressions of long-term historical processes.

To the question as to how one may comprehend long-term historical processes for as complex an entity as contemporary India, many of whose strands go back into *European* history, there is no easy answer. Ordinary descriptive procedures would quickly draw one into infinitely diverse, unmanageable detail. My procedure in these pages, instead, will be to construct a model, an exercise in which the central tactic has to be to deliberately simplify situations known to be highly complex; this is done in order to focus on what is judged to be essential or more consequential for the purposes at hand—omitting attention to the lesser elements. Paradoxically, it is my grounding in *anthropology* which appears to have equipped me with the elementary habits of mind which have gone into this effort (Saberwal 1985: 237ff gives an account). My sense of the historical dimension in the shaping of societies has grown through my location in the Centre for Historical Studies at Jawaharlal Nehru University. Convergent with this influence have been others from within anthropology and sociology (see p. 4n), linked with such names as Max Weber, Clifford Geertz, and Victor Turner. (Turner was my teacher whose example both in personal relationships and in scholarship remains a point of reference.)

The three substantive chapters in this work are modestly revised versions of papers published earlier. In their original versions, the treatments in Chapter 2 and 3 were somewhat overlapping. This overlap has now been reduced, and Chapter 3 carries the argument a step further. Chapter 4 had to be recast to secure consistency of format. During this tinkering I have attended to several errors and infelicities of style also, but the arguments remain essentially as published initially. This work is addressed primarily to the Indian reader who is assumed to be as unfamiliar with European history as I was until 1980. Consequently, Chapter 2 abounds in citations for events which may be common knowledge for other readers. To these latter, my apologies.

Chapter 4, on communalism, is based on a paper written in 1980 during sabbatical leave from Jawaharlal Nehru University. This theme dissolved for me later into the larger issue of social crisis, examined during a fellowship at Nehru Memorial Museum and Library, New Delhi (1982–4). To this issue, political traditions appeared to be central, and these were discussed in a paper published in 1984 (Chapter 3). A statement on my overall framework (Chapter 2) appeared the next year. In arranging the papers for this work, I have reversed the order of their initial writing. (I should add that I expect to amplify this discussion to a more adequate scale later in this decade.)

When published originally, these papers recorded my many debts then; and over the years these debts have continued to grow. Ecumenical Christian Centre, Bangalore, and Vidya Jyoti, Delhi, have given me vitally useful hospitality. The University Grants

Commission asked me to deliver its National Lectures in sociology during 1985–6, and the themes in this work were part of the series. My many friends at Punjab University and at the Universities of Jodhpur, Hyderabad, and Poona did much to make my visits there both instructive and pleasurable. Rajiv Lochan, Harbans Mukhia, K. N. Panikkar, Majid Siddiqi and my editor at the Oxford University Press (who insists on anonymity) have been generous in advice and criticism. My family has continued to forbear my curious enthusiasms which often pass into obsessions, and I am grateful.

For permission to adapt previously published material, specific acknowledgements are due: for Chapter 2, which adapts 'Modelling the crisis: megasociety, multiple codes, and social blanks', to *Economic and Political Weekly* (1985, 20: 202–11); for Chapter 3, which adapts 'On the social crisis in India: political traditions', to *Contributions to Indian Sociology* (1984, 18: 63–84); for Chapter 4, which adapts 'Elements of communalism', to the Director, Nehru Memorial Museum and Library (*Mainstream*, March 21 and 28, 1981); and for parts of Chapter 1, which draw on 'Analysing the Indian social crisis: a personal chronicle', to *Journal of Social and Economic Studies* (1985, n.s. 2: 224–41) and Sage Publications (India) Pvt. Ltd., New Delhi.

Jawaharlal Nehru University   Satish Saberwal
14 April 1986

CHAPTER 1

INTRODUCTION

I

Until the early 1950s the 'book view' of Indian society was dominant in sociology in India: it sought to analyse texts, principally of the Hindu tradition, for principles informing the distinctively Indian social institutions—the caste system, family relationships, worldviews, etc.—and underlying it was the Durkheimian stress on the importance of relatively stable ideas, of forms of consciousness, within a tradition. During the 1950s it gave way to the 'field view', stressing the primacy of observational data, arising in the course of anthropological fieldwork: and this happened for rather simple reasons. It had influential Anglo-American sponsors. Leaving aside the difference this could make to the personal life chances of many among those who would follow them in India, it had the advantage too in appealing to the self-evident truth of one's own— or the sociologist's own—observations, as against the truth of writings that were millennia old.

Furthermore, at least in more skilful hands, the observational data were not seen atomistically; rather, from these points of departure, particular acts had to be located in relation to other acts, beliefs, institutions—all assumed to be interrelated functionally. That is to say, acts were seen in context, in the context of a social *field*: a village, a neighbourhood, and the like. This enterprise sought to locate the field in its larger contexts too: one thinks of Srinivas's distinction between local, regional, peninsular, and all-India Hinduism (1952: Ch. 7), or Redfield's between the Little and the Great Traditions (1956). It tended, however, to bracket the colonial phase off into omnibus categories like 'westernization'—specified with trait-lists at best—without situating these in *their* historical context adequately. (Mukherjee, 1977, has an overview.)

Over the past decade I have found myself gradually pushed towards what might be called a 'world historical view' of Indian society. It would seek to analyse observational fields by way not

2   INDIA : THE ROOTS OF CRISIS

merely of their internal, synchronic interrelatedness but also of the
long-term clash and confluence of ideas, institutional forms, and
patterns of conduct arising in different traditions—seen to be
located in their historical time. This view has arisen for me in a
conjunction of impulses which are partly autobiographical, beginning in the 1950s; partly institutional, with my location in the
Centre for Historical Studies, Jawaharlal Nehru University since
1973; and partly disciplinary, by way of recovering, successively,
different strands from the sociological tradition. I have recently
examined at some length these several sets of impulses going into
my developing sense of the problem (1985); we need not repeat
that account here. We shall consider here, instead, the premises
underlying the arguments in the three studies which follow, con-
centrating on some of the less familiar concepts and premises and
noticing the interlinkages between the apparently disparate directions of these several arguments.

II

Chapter 2 offers my overall argument, bringing this world historical view to bear upon the crisis in contemporary Indian society.
It sees this crisis as a consequence of our collective difficulty in
working with institutions of Western derivation which have been
implanted in India during and after the colonial period: legislatures, courts, universities, banks and so forth. Our difficulty arises
perhaps in a lack of fit between the principles which have gone
into the designing of these institutions, over many long centuries
in Europe, and those which inform institutions to which we in
India have traditionally been heir: family, caste, village, pilgrimage centre, little kingdom, and so forth.

A sense of this contrast has indeed been a sociological commonplace, echoing repeatedly the late nineteenth century categories
associated with Henry Maine, Ferdinand Toennies, and others.
Central for us, however, is the circumstance that these sets of
institutions stand to each other in a relationship not merely of
contrast but also of *conjunction*: forms of institutions brought into
conjunction during the colonial phase and continuing to inter-
penetrate since then. Consequently, we can now examine the
nature of difficulties in controlling and running these Western
institutions, after a generation's experience of doing so indepen-

dently. It is necessary to take these essentially Weberian questions very much more seriously now than was the case, say, in the 1960s, when these were first broached in India, principally in relation to the prospects of capitalist development.

The colonially implanted arrangements made a difference to society in India. The arrangements which made a difference were partly technical, as with the railways, and partly social, as with the bureaucracy or the regime of capitalism; and the persistent, *cumulative* consequence of these arrangements was that they facilitated the *enlargement of the potentially effective scales of social relationships.*[1] This consequence has been especially striking in the context of the relatively small-scale social universes marking a society whose segmentedness has had no parallel in history. This enlargement of scales can be seen in various domains: in the magnitudes of personal travel; in the magnitudes of trade and, from the mid-1800s on, of industrial production; in the magnitudes of participation in the routines for political legitimation, say in elections for legislatures; and so forth. To refer summarily to this techno-social order, resulting from the European, colonial presence in India, I shall use the term 'megasociety'.

By the 1950s there was a considerable literature in anthropology (e.g., SSRC 1954) examining the implications of the overwhelming Western presence for the indigenes in the Americas, in Africa, and elsewhere; and the Western habit of searching for general propositions to accommodate particular observed cases has yielded formulations which bear on our problem too (Bidney 1946; Wallace 1957, 1961: 143–64). The difficulties in contemporary India cannot, however, be attributed to an overwhelming presence of alien forces, even though some of our public figures do at times see the 'foreign hand' in any disorder they are unable otherwise to explain. Nor does the crisis lie in a general personal sense of disorientation, though that may be growing. The sources of our difficulties are rather different.

Undergirded by the Roman Catholic Church and working with still older cultural resources, such as Greek logic and Roman legal techniques, European societies moved during the middle ages towards a unification of codes which facilitated an enlarging of

---

[1]See, Saberwal 1979: 253ff. The notion is an old one. See Ch. 2: Scale, in Godfrey and Monica Wilson, 1945.

4 INDIA : THE ROOTS OF CRISIS

operative scales, culminating in the megasocieties of our time. Colonialism fitted India with a techno-social frame of comparable scale for its own purposes; but the highly segmented Indian social space had carried a multiplicity of codes: each segment—*jati*—functioning in terms of its own more or less distinctive code, its own normative order, which was once subject to regulation principally from within the group. As these diverse codes flow into megasocietal institutions, the latter move towards breakdown. We have tended to take the maintenance of such institutions for granted, but this assumption is now ripe for very serious scrutiny. The maintaining and the renewing of a megasociety calls for a range of institutional capabilities whose weakness or absence among Indians I shall call 'social blanks'. I shall suggest that these social blanks may account for India's difficulties with the task that history has set it.

III

Readers unfamiliar with the social sciences may be disconcerted by a style of analysis which banks on ideas and institutions from centuries and even millennia past to explain a contemporary situation. Underlying the studies in this work is the general proposition that complex societal processes may have notable continuities over the long term[2] even though, at other levels, the same society may be changing noticeably. Georges Gurvitch, the French sociologist, notices (1971) multiple levels or layers in societal phenomena: some lying 'deeper' than others in the sense partly of controlling the shallower levels and partly of being less amenable to changes over the short run. Many would maintain, for example, that the princi-

[2]Societal continuities over the long term have found strong recognition in recent decades from varied standpoints. The term *la longue durée* comes from Fernand Braudel, the historian of early modern Europe; and Guenther Roth (1979) has drawn a correspondence between his vision and that of Max Weber who examined, comparatively, the ideas and institutions which mediate in the long-term continuity of societies. The play of 'deeply sedimented time-space relations' in the events of the passing moment (Giddens 1979: 110) would be examined also in the Geertzian 'thick description' (1973); and there are resonances here with the search for the enduring structures of ideas and their expression in observable events (thus, Dumont 1957), such as appear, in another kind of analytic context, as Victor Turner's 'root paradigms' (1974).

ple of hierarchy is layered deeply in the Indian tradition in a manner that the rule of impersonal law is not.

This work assumes furthermore that, in coping with one's objective reality, an actor works with what cultural resources may be available. While some such resources may be devised or adapted to answer particular contingencies, the premise here is that, in any functioning social order, such capacities are not infinitely plastic. Even in large societies, key choices once made affect the society overall in the long run, enabling, inhibiting, influencing, or canalizing much subsequent conduct and choice. A core of such ideas, cultural resources, and associated institutions defines a tradition, giving it consistency.

Viewed from the actor's standpoint, these elements in the tradition would not determine one's actions directly or in detail. It is, rather, that the actor, in search of possible ways for acting—and for legitimating one's actions—would turn to these elements in the antecedent tradition. These elements, even though excluded from the formal public charters of the day, may have continued to be available in some social institutions, in folklore, in socialization practices and so forth. Contrariwise, other elements whose availability these formal charters might take for granted may in fact not be available in the actor's effective social and cultural milieu;[3] and in that case his or her conduct in relation to the charters would be problematical.

The third premise underlying this work, especially in Chapters 2 and 3, is comparative; our understanding of an entity can advance, *inter alia*, by comparing it with other entities of a similar order. The principal comparisons here will refer to aspects of the Indian and European traditions. Comparisons in this vein have repeatedly been drawn by Western scholars, Weber and Dumont among the sociologists, and the possibility has been hinted at by Indian scholars too (e.g. Tripathi 1964: 153ff; M. Habib 1981: 362). In the following chapters we consider (1) the processes marking the two traditions comparatively and (2) the implications of the historic conjoining of institutions—which arose independently in the two traditions.

---

[3]The discussion of 'institutionalization' below (pp. 31) will examine this issue from another angle.

IV

Out of the wide canvas of this comparison in Chapter 2, the next chapter comes to focus on the institutions of power and authority. The centrality of power and authority in shaping the course of a society has in recent years had to be recognized afresh in contexts as diverse as early modern European history (Anderson 1974: 35f, n. 4); medieval South Indian history (Appadurai 1981: 8; Dirks 1976: 126); contemporary theory of 'development' (Das Gupta 1981); and general sociological theory (Giddens 1979: 68 *et al.*). This is a convergent reaction to diverse earlier tendencies, ranging from the functionalist accentuation of the normative to the Marxist accentuation of the economic.

As between societies, institutions of power and authority have varied over a very wide range historically. Activities, experiences and expectations characterizing a society are set, in varying measure, by the forms and capacities of these political institutions; and these are especially important in complex societies of large scale wherein diverse activities, spread widely over time and space, need mutual order and co-ordination. We have noted that constitutive ideas—that is, cultural resources—are central to durable institutions generally and this applies also to institutions of power and authority; yet it is in the operation of institutions that the strength of ideas is expressed and commitment to them renewed, and so the institutions need to be examined in their own right too. This will be attempted in Chapter 3.

Put otherwise, political institutions are critical because these set the terms, as it were, on which all kinds of activities—political, scholarly, managerial, or whatever—can or cannot proceed. A crisis in political institutions spawns far reaching uncertainties and anxieties: one need think only of events in India between 1975 and 1980 or of the aftermath of Mrs Gandhi's assassination. Acute difficulties in the working of political institutions have recently been endemic in several Indian states also. The designs of these institutions—such as those established by the Constitution—have been taken largely from Western prototypes. In most cases, the *scales* of these institutions are much larger than the scales of functioning which have been customary to the indigenous institutions. The inner logic of these institutions of imported designs may not always be clear to those whose actions are critical to their maintenance; and the decay of institutions which constitute a domain must sooner or later lead to crisis—or worse.

This enlargement of scales appears to offer the key for interpreting another expression of crisis too, namely, the *rise of communalism* during and after the colonial period. Chapter 4 approaches the issue of communalism via the nature of social identities, especially religious identities. Much of the discussion there turns on an elementary question: why do religious beliefs, which are often weak on empirical validity, inspire confidence among the believers and, furthermore, why do communal identities command the allegiance even of a good many *un*believers? I shall argue that the compulsions of having to cope with the enlargement of scales during the colonial period and after have necessitated widespread redefinitions of the boundaries of the groups of one's allegiance; and this redefinition has commonly meant that, as the generations have turned over, the earlier sense of identity—often in terms of limited segments of a caste group and the like—has tended to give way to larger identities—in terms of religious boundaries which encapsulate the earlier identities of smaller scale. The play of communal identities has had to compete with that of other identities of various shapes and sizes, including those associated with nationalism. Yet it is the communal identities which have often carried the day in the Indian marketplace of social identities; and Chapter 4 seeks to identify the elements requisite for explaining why.

V

It may be appropriate to note here that, as a domain for serious scholarly analysis, the phenomenon of communalism has tended to be neglected over the decades. More effort has been bestowed on it in recent years but there are severe disagreements over what exactly the issue for analysis is and what the rules of the game are for proceeding with this analysis (Ch. 4 below). Why should this be so?

I would suggest that our major *analytic* difficulty with communalism lies in the fact that it is *not* an *ordered* phenomenon. The peaceable formulae associated with Akbar, Kabir, Gandhi, etc. concerning inter-religious relationships have been too elementary, and too devoid of institutional muscle, to cope with the situations on the ground over the long term. To make the point, we may compare communalism with the caste system. The caste system as it functioned in village India, say up to a generation ago, was an outcome of several millennia of efforts at *social ordering*, efforts which were organized and directed with reference to an elaborate ideology. The Brahminical ideology was encompassing, willing to accommodate everyone in its design which provided for a great deal besides a model for village organization.

Communalism, to be sure, has its ideologies, but these are *partial* ideologies, such as those proferred by the Rashtriya Swayamsevak Sangh, Jamaat-i-Islami, All-India Sikh Students Federation, and sundry other organizations. One cannot find an ideology for organizing anything like a 'communal system' in an orderly manner. This is so because each religious tradition lays claim to being sovereign in itself, to possessing the Truth exclusively.[4] Furthermore, as the followers of the partial ideologies of communalism act out their logics, this generates not social order but, rather, social *dis*order, at times riotously.

It so happens that general analytic models concerning situations of disorder are much less readily available than those for previously ordered phenomena. For coming to grips with such phenomena, then, it is necessary to track down what it is that generates such disorder. In my analysis of communalism, its specific capacity for generating disorder is seen to arise in these partial ideologies, which are constructed around religious identities. And to make sense of religious identities, it is essential that these be located in the context of the respective religious traditions.

In concluding these introductory comments, I would like to draw attention to the sparsity of adequate scholarship on not only the phenomenon of communalism but also on the more general one of the social crisis in contemporary India. I attribute this sparsity also to the situation that the myriad expressions of crisis, in turn, are *not ordered* phenomena. Proceeding again on the premise that in such situations it is necessary to track down the founts that generate the disorder, and recognizing the imperative to locate one's analytic units parsimoniously, the overall framework in

---

[4]In contrast, the groups constituting the caste system have traditionally submitted, willy nilly, to its overall ideology.

Chapter 2 argues that the contemporary situation is best seen as an outcome of the conjunction between long term, contrasting, historical processes in India and Europe. Such a framework has not found much favour with scholars in India, but the issue appears to invite reconsideration.

MEGASOCIETY, MULTIPLE CODES, AND SOCIAL BLANKS

I

The mayhem following Mrs Gandhi's assassination served as a shocking reminder of the social crisis enveloping India. It has been common to see the crisis principally in economic and political terms (e.g., Frankel 1978, Kothari 1983, Manor 1983). The next chapter will consider the issue comparatively, with reference to medieval Indian political institutions viewed over the long term and the European political tradition. The present chapter moves from such *comparison* to the consequences of colonial *conjunction*, widening the focus on to the overall sociocultural domain, a domain encompassing the strictly political. In anthropological parlance, my focus is on 'culture', a term to be considered explicitly in Chapter 4.

To gain perspective, it is useful to recall that Europe has often experienced a sense of crisis over the past centuries. Trevor-Roper identified a 'general crisis' in the *seventeenth* century, issuing from several convergent strands. The state's monopoly over taxes and over public force; its access to better cannon, to the use of gunpowder, and to specialist, better trained and better commanded armies: all enhanced the power at the centre of the state to a point where historians of the late medieval and early modern Europe designate these as absolutist states. This enabled the states both to breach the cities' traditional autonomy at home and to underwrite imperial expansion, initially in the Americas. The consequent expansion of the bureaucracies stretched the states' finances to the point of making them sell their offices as a source of revenue, yielding an increasingly parasitic bureaucracy. It took a series of upheavals—including the English revolution of the mid-1600s—to clear the consequent 'crisis in the relations between society and the State' (Trevor-Roper 1967: 55, *passim*; Anderson 1974: Ch. 1).

The nineteenth century had to cope with the consequences of two revolutions: one political, the French, the other economic, the industrial revolution, and these gave Europe a sense of disorientation acute enough for its scholars to go scurrying for more adequate conceptions of the bases of society: 'How is society possible?' asked Georg Simmel, the German philosopher, in a famous passage (1908). During the inter-War years of the twentieth century, the rise of Hitler and of his pogroms was an obvious and very grave threat to civilized existence. The consequent effort to reconstitute the basic meanings that men and women may live by was led in England by a rising generation of writers, sometimes called the Auden generation, after their leading poet. More recently, as the United States sought to bomb Vietnam into the stone age, a fresh cultural crisis engulfed the West, illustrated in the student revolt in Paris in May 1968. Recalling these crises, it is useful to remember the durable Western skills in reconstituting meanings, significances, and institutions as part of the effort to cope with the successive crises. We need to be familiar with their historical record even though our crisis has strikingly different parameters.

II

Colonialism brought England, part of Europe, into conjunction with the various societies in the Indian subcontinent. Sharply contrasted principles of social organization had informed the designing of the two traditions historically; but the conjunction changed the context for Indian societies rather abruptly. A major dimension of this change was to introduce a long-term tendency towards enlarging the *sociotechnical frame*; that is, the framework constituted both by *material* technology, including the physical means of communication, such as the railways, and by *social* technology, including the administrative arrangements which constituted the colonial regime. Given, furthermore, the monopoly over force which the colonial state could impose, there was the possibility of a dramatic physical dispersal—whose other face was social expansion—of such groups as the Marwaris and the Syrian Christians. Rather more varied and complex career paths became available, at least to small social fractions, than had previously been the case, although, as everyone knows, this process lay within a larger one of colonial domination and exploitation.

This capacity for enlarging the technical frame, and with that the scale of possible social relationships, had accrued to Western Europe

over long centuries. Something of the temporal depth of the processes underneath may be grasped by noting that a sense of large-
scale political order marked Ancient Rome which, two thousand
years ago, had presided over one of the greatest empires known to
man. The Empire waned later; but its memory was kept alive in the
Christian monasteries of the early medieval years—say the sixth to
the tenth centuries—and transmitted to the new political regimes
then rising in Europe.

The growth of monasteries during and after the sixth century
was one expression of the continuity of a religious tradition
embodied in the Catholic church centred in Rome. Expanding
gradually to become an institution of continental reach, the
importance of the Church in European history was at its greatest
between the decline of the Roman Empire, especially after the fifth
century, and the fourteenth century, by which time several European
states had become firmly established while the church itself began
to get into serious difficulties. During the intervening period, the
church carried, now passively, now actively, a tradition with several
discrete strands. First, the Greek apparatus for systematic thought,
available partially until the thirteenth century, when there were
major further accruals in translations both from Arab sources in
Spain and directly from Greek (Piltz 1981: 174–86). Second, the
Christian religious traditions, with its relatively simple interpersonal
ethic and its attack both on exclusive, wide-ranging kinship and
on magical practices (Weber 1950: 50, 238, 265; 1968: 579–80).
These elements were central to the texts and the theology of the
church. The third element drew upon the Roman search for
bureaucratic forms of organization under the Emperors (Hopkins
1968). It is this last strand which enabled the church itself to grow
into an institution of vast scale and durability which could provide
post-Roman Europe with something of a *political* framework as well.

Amidst the debris of the Roman Empire, what the church was
able to do, in effect, was to keep these various elements of a crucial
tradition alive in its own awareness. Apart from the small, peri-
pheral Jewish communities, and—in southern parts—Islamic ones,
the Roman Catholic church came to exercise a virtual monopoly
over the *symbolic order*.[1] The consequently shared symbolic order
underlay a sense of the community at various rungs of social

---

[1] For a general feel of this monopoly, see Duby (1980 and 1981).

organization. Through the centuries its organizational scale would enable the church to smother the many heresies—at least until Martin Luther could begin using the printing press. A major source of strength for the church lay in the numerous monasteries which combined prayer with manual labour and with learning in changing combinations. These monastic orders were important not only in maintaining a religious and cultural tradition but also in varied agricultural and other technological developments in Europe during the second half of the first millennium (Cipolla 1972, especially papers by G. Duby and L. White Jr.): these developments contributed to an expansion of operational scales.

We have noted the deep roots of the Church in the Western tradition; the idea of the state came to acquire similar roots in the early medieval centuries. Charlemagne was crowned Emperor in Rome in A.D. 800 in an act which inaugurated the Holy Roman Empire, consciously recalling the Roman legacy. Latin was the effective, international language of the church; and since literacy did not go much beyond the church, it was men of the church who were often pressed into roles crucial for the conduct of the state too (Bloch 1961: 157, 422 *passim*). Europe's emperors and kings in subsequent centuries were anointed by the church, as were the bishops. The kings were also bishops of the church, anointed to rule on earth parts of what was held to be the larger kingdom of Jesus. Heirs to the throne were expected to receive instruction similar to that given to future bishops, and it included much meditation on Latin texts on the ancient Roman Empire (Duby 1981: Ch. 1). In fashioning the key political institutions during this period, thus, the church's role was critically constitutive. It is from this deep layering within the tradition that such institutions as the church and the state acquired their enduring hold over the larger society.

Late in the eleventh century, however, the terms of the relationship between the sacred and the secular orders—which included the question of control over vast church properties—came under protracted contention, a contest known as the Investiture Struggle. Thomas Beckett's encounter with Henry II of England in the 1160s, culminating in the murder in the cathedral, was one episode in a controlled, persistent struggle which continued into the early 1200s. (Later centuries brought their own bones of contention, but these need not detain us here.) In their search for levers of possible advantage, the contestants during the late eleventh and twelfth centuries turned to the study of the legal tradition—both canon law and the older, secular Roman legacy (Tellenbach 1940: 102, 115; Piltz 1981: 65 *et seqq.*).

The Roman sense of political order had included the social technology of constructing legal codes. Their use in Rome had been rather limited, but their study had been maintained in Ravenna (Ullmann 1955: 367f), a coastal town in north-eastern Italy, which had become the locus of imperial control from Constantinople following the decline of Rome. These skills were revived, beginning with the late eleventh century. As the utility of the Roman legal devices in bringing order and consistency to the expanding range of economic, political, and social relationships—within the church as well as outside—became clear, the learning of that legal tradition moved from Ravenna into secular institutions which became established as universities by the thirteenth century.

Kings all over Western Europe took avidly to this technology of law as part of constituting a framework for administering justice in their domains. Confidence in the justice administered by kings' secular courts has recently been seen by Eric Jones (1981: 233) as crucial in binding securely the loyalty of European subjects to their kings. The point to remember is that Roman Law, inclined to propositions of maximal generality, was part of an ancient tradition native to Europe. In the emergent situation, its constitutive ideas needed only to be revived; these did not have to be invented from scratch, nor grafted from a radically alien tradition.

The study of law was only one of the fields going into the making of the early universities, such as that in Paris. The Greek philosophical tradition had existed in parts, in limited Latin translations, in the early medieval monasteries; but the resources for systematic thought available to the church grew dramatically in the late twelfth century through infusion of a much larger Greek corpus acquired both from the Arabs and from Greece. Philosophy and theology, consequently, were the two other fields cultivated at these early universities (Murray 1978: Ch. 12, *passim*; Duby 1981: 145ff). The church for its own reasons helped the universities establish *their* autonomy (see Piltz 1981: 129 on the University of Paris in 1215),[2] a matter of jurisdiction over which churchmen and kings

---

[2]Le Goff (1980: 135–49) examines the relationship of the universities with public authorities through the 1500s.

had been arguing for several generations since the 1070s. Precedents for the later autonomy of institutions—the basis of professionalism—were being laid here, but the importance of this autonomy was immediate. The Aristotelian apparatus for drawing inferences allowed for consistency in thought from given premises; but a divergence of premises was also possible under academic autonomy, and so there followed a diversity of intellectual constructs built on the divergent premises: the careers of Thomas Aquinas, Duns Scotus, and William of Occam among others presaged the variety of viewpoints to arise in the early modern period (Piltz 1981 : 159–260). This is noteworthy, even though it would take several centuries yet to make a dent in popular beliefs and world-views (Thomas 1971).

The role of the church in the shaping of Europe, then, was decisive. It had given the society a certain institutional continuity in a period of grave political breakdown. The clerics served for centuries in the conduct of the state's administration and diplomacy.[3] It constructed a unified cultural tradition out of disparate materials, and made a common ethic effectively available throughout the continent. It helped establish the habit of reasoning in secular institutions of learning, including the universities, charged with 'carrying out the continuous social function of training a large proportion of the ruling classes in rational analysis' (Holmes 1975: 135). The lasting value of these institutions, established firmly in the Western tradition early in the second millennium, became all the clearer as the Church itself entered a phase of decline after 1300.

III

Yet other processes contributing to the growth of operational scales in Europe were centred on *commerce* and *shipping*, activities which were much accelerated by the experience of the Crusades between the late 1000s and the mid-1200s. Sailings of growing reach came gradually to connect the West Asian ports—in the Black Sea and the Mediterranean—with North European ports in the Baltic; and with this went the growing habit of testing reality, both physical and social, as we shall see shortly. These sailings

---

[3]Buck (1983) studies this interconnection in early fourteenth-century England.

were carriers principally of trade; and as the scale of trade grew, the Italian merchants' search for advantage led them (1) to abandon Roman numerals in favour of Arabic numerals, which were taken from Arab traders; these Arabic numerals helped greatly in simplifying relatively complex problems in commercial arithmetic, especially those of multiplication and division (Murray 1978: Ch. 7); and (2) to devise the double-entry system of book-keeping (1340 or earlier: Scammell 1981: 205). Altogether, these several strands helped augment the Europeans' skill in calculative reasoning, which was so central to the long-term rise of capitalism.

Associated with all this, one can identify a more general skill—that of the *accurate* recognition of external reality, social as well as physical, so that there could be general agreement on the characteristics of that reality; and there was also a gradual recognition, that action in terms of these accurate, agreed characteristics tended to attain its goal, avoiding mishap. The most dramatic expression of this orientation to reality was to be seen, of course, in Europe's mastery of the oceans and in its ability, 1492 on, to penetrate every continent and every island on this earth. It included a growing capacity to organize information about that reality into useable form, say, sailing charts for jagged coastlines, and directions for sailing the oceans (ibid., 206–8). And it included technological skills for manipulating that reality to advantage: *watermills* and *windmills*, harnessing inanimate energy (White 1972: 156f; Thrupp 1972: 232ff); a burst of monumental *cathedral building* (1100s to early 1300s), whose architecture sought to make scholastic points by way of intricate geometric analyses (Duby 1981: 149); *guns* and gunpowder; *reading glasses*, invented in Venice in the 1290 (Murray 1978: 302) often doubling a person's years of active reading; *clocks*, in the 1300s, facilitating the organization of one's own time, and co-ordination with others (White 1972: 160; le Goff 1972: 86ff); *printing*, which by the early 1500s could enable Erasmus to become the first man to live on the market earnings from his books, and Luther to defy the might of the Church (White 1972: 160f; Johnson 1976: 169–86); and so forth.

Medieval Europe achieved a similar orientation towards *social* reality too. The penetration of continents was not done by guns alone; it relied also on active routines for ascertaining the social reality, including estimates of magnitudes of likely threats from hostile peoples around you. It called for the less warlike social skills also. During the 1600s, Mughal power was at its peak and European consolidations along the Indian coasts were not achieved by out-gunning the Mughals. It took complex *skills for learning the skills* appropriate to the varied social and cultural milieus in which they found themselves.

An early sensitivity to the social context is evident in numerous other ways too. In the mid-1200s, the Mongols were knocking at the doors of Europe in the East. First the Pope, Innocent IV, and then the king of France, Louis IX, sent emissaries—Franciscan monks—to the court of the great Khan of the Mongols in Karakorum to ascertain what kind of society they had, and what their intentions were towards the Muslims, the Christians, and so forth (Southern 1962: 44–51). (In contrast, during the seventeenth and eighteenth centuries, our ancestors in India made very little serious attempt to judge what the long-term intentions of Europeans in India could be.) In India, the records produced by Europeans—travellers and merchants—are a major resource for the history of the medieval period.

European capabilities by this time, however, reached well beyond observing and recording, and day-to-day coping; these included systematic administrative rearrangements too, seen in the Venetian and Genoese mini-empires in Greece and West Asia during the late medieval centuries (Scammell 1981: Chs. 3 and 4) and in the rise of absolutist states at home. Such gradually constructed skills and capabilities lay at the heart of the British bid for the mastery of India.

We have a multiple convergence here: of the shared symbolic order and the consequent sense of community; of the administration of justice and the consequent attachment to rulers; of the growing skills—with consistency in argument, with testing reality both physical and social, and with calculative reasoning. Commensurate with the slow, internally propelled institutional evolution and technological growth were adjustments in attitudes and orientations and banks of ideas. Beneath these several elements there are shared styles of thought and action, making for that *unification of codes* which has underlain the European capacity for organized action of growing scope, a capacity ultimately expressed, in part, in the techno-social frames constructed in the Empires. These were specific personal skills, transmitted in a particular, more or less institutionalized context, and in particular forms of historically achieved social relationships. How well and stably these could be transplanted in other culture-historical settings is a question whose answer is sought best not in *a priori* argument but in the course of history which we are now able to scrutinize.

The enlargement of the technical frame, during and after the colonial period, has meant that we in India have taken over Western material technology willingly; we have also taken at least the forms—the shells—of some Western institutions like the university; but we have had very serious difficulties, once you move away from tiny metropolitan islets, with making commensurate adjustments in—with redefining and reconceptualizing—attitudes, orientations, and ideas. We have noticed that Europe was fortunate in having had deeply layered institutional traditions which nurtured the attitudes and the styles appropriate to society on the scale it was attaining—and in which, more or less involuntarily, we find ourselves, but *without* the comparable institutions which are requisite to meet the imperatives of our time.

IV

The Indian historical experience stands in remarkable contrast to the European. Viewed over the *large* scale, there are discontinuities (see Chapter 3): in spatial extent (as with Rajput kingdoms or the Cholas), in temporal duration (as with the Mughals), or in both, with the more ephemeral units. Alongside this political fragility over time and space, there has often tended also to be considerable discontinuity in the symbolic order and in the key social stratum controlling the state, illustrated by the gaps between the Rajputs and the Saltanat (see Chapter 3). This difference with Europe can be attributed to the absence in India of a master institution, such as the Roman Catholic Church, which demonstrated, historically, an unparalleled, organized capacity for maintaining internal institutional purpose and coherence amidst surrounding political and social fragmentariness. This internal institutional continuity enabled it to give endogenic social and political processes relatively steady direction in Europe.

Over the large scale, then, *the Indian polity has had a jerky, discontinuous career*; but *on the small scale, Indian society has shown notable continuity*. I refer to the social universe—admittedly a severely segmented social universe—in which *most* people *most* of the time would be encapsulated within the small world of family, caste, and village. Within this small universe, ordinarily there was considerable continuity, and security, from one generation to the next. The legacy of that small-scale, segmented social universe lives with us—even in most institutions of the metropolitan centres, often in ways unbeknown to us—and it will stay with us for a very long time, however resolutely we try to wish it away. It behoves us, therefore, to take it squarely into account.

The world of that local universe is familiar and easily sketched. A hierarchy of multiple caste groups, set apart in conception, in kinship, and in specified interactions, yet intertwined in the local agricultural cycle, in ritual, and in relations of dominance. Mobilization for dominance, which meant control over productive resources, especially land, was caste-centred in the first instance, and the dominance of a caste—Rajputs, Jats, Vallalas—could reach as wide as a region; but the loyalties of caste could not stretch beyond the region, nor, therefore, could polities resting on these loyalties.[4] The ongoing *social* order was set in established forms of inter-caste relations, sustained by the authority of the dominant caste or the raja, an authority whose assertion—by applying force—would be needed only occasionally. Beyond the locality, there were the links of kinship and marriage, pilgrimage and tribute to a superior ruler, and in some areas commercial production and trade; but these latter would be links of limited social content. The social ties of urban groups active in commerce, or in the conduct of the state, would be more extensive and durable; but even there the horizons of personal relations were set in important ways by the bounds of one's caste.[5]

The raja and the town loomed large in the wider scene, but the context which framed a person's life, with praise and with sanction, was principally that of the family and the caste group. The

[4]True, these 'regions' were often larger than many states in Europe. The point is that the difficulty with political mobilization noted here applied principally to the *endogenic* political efforts. External political entrepreneurs—carrying distinctive religious identities—could construct much larger states, subordinating the indigenous polities. This entailed discontinuities in political institutions on one hand and yet further segmentation of society on the other.

[5]Mandelbaum (1970) provides an introduction to the structure of Indian society and carries a useful bibliography.

latter, especially, tended to be more or less autonomous, its members being subject to its internal control, very much more so than to the controls originating with the state or with other external authority. The burden of socializing—that is, of canalizing the impulses of the young—was carried very largely by kin and caste-mates in terms of their understanding of their lived-in reality. To limit this discussion to the Hindu tradition, a larger social vision, or an organized, wider institutional presence reaching into the locality, has not been very active in sharing this burden with primary groups, like the family.

Whatever our prized sacred texts may say, the ethic operative behind segmental confines has tended to be particular to the segment, not general or universal; most people, most of the time, were enclosed in relatively limited, specified interactions, and in any case did not need very much by way of a generalized, universal code. The society got by with but sporadic institutional arrangements—say the itinerant *sadhu*—for propagating a general ethic. Religious contexts—pilgrimages, temples for worship— brought the devotee into settings organized as, and defined to be, sacred; but this sacredness did not attach itself to a commonly available universal ethic. Within this overall framework tended to fit the other religious traditions—Jain, Muslim, Sikh, Christian— when they added to the complexity of the locality.

The limiting of the operative ethics to segmental boundaries may be seen another way. Granting the reflective nature of the human being as an attribute of the species, one which strains after consistency (Berger and Luckmann 1966: 160, 181 *et al.*), this reflectiveness in India would seem to have been canalized in a particular way. Malamoud (1981) has noticed that the tradition recognizes shifts in the relative ordering of the goals of life—*puruṣarthas*— from one *varna* to another; this stance appears on the ground in the caste groups' substantial normative autonomy (Mandelbaum 1970: Chap. 13), an autonomy which extended also to other kinds of social categories encapsulated in caste-like social spaces in the caste order. This cellular universe has traditionally seemed to accept separate, more or less insulated social spaces relatively easily, often in a *both/and* rather than an *either/or* logic (R. Mukherjee 1970: 1160–5; M. Singer 1972: 321–5), so that the social order accommodated strikingly contrasting forms of conduct in its different parts (but see p. 22).

Should the primacy of one or the other logic in a particular context be at issue, such determination would have rested with the area's royal figure; and should the ruler not be available, being non-Hindu, an alternative locus for authoritative determination could be devised, as with *jati* councils in fourteenth-century Bengal (Inden 1976: 77f).

These *order-maintaining routines* were associated with, and effective in, a social milieu marked with (1) rather modest scales of physical and social mobility, and (2) an acceptance of the caste order as axiomatic, an acceptance which legitimized a variety of segmental codes of conduct. Diverse codes of conduct were legitimized for different social categories in this social order; and these were insulated mutually, facing one another only in relatively set, stereotyped situations in customary ways. When the particular forms of conduct crossed their established social bounds, order-maintaining routines were available which could be invoked to determine the precedence of particular forms. The working of these routines was context-sensitive[6]: it would weigh the nuances of power and influence effective in the particular setting, rather than try to impose general rules over-riding such nuances. Reinforcing this sense of order were the rituals of community within a locality, which might help hold its several strands together, if only to stress the locality's community of interests *vis-a-vis* the agencies of the state.

Whatever the rituals of community in the locality, however, the locus of sociological reality—by way of identities, of active relations of kinship, affinity and ritual, and of operative norms—rested in the caste group, as Dumont and Pocock (1957: 26f) noticed a generation ago. Each caste group had set its own norms, its own codes, as to what is right and what is wrong, without much reference to larger societal codes, except on such points as hierarchy and purity (though when disputes were taken to the locally dominant caste for settlement, the latter's will would prevail). These codes had tended to be attuned to a group's traditional occupation: scavenger, warrior, merchant, official, priest. In view of the severely limited, though not unknown, movement *between* occupations, the processes of social mobility did not much compromise the separation of the segmental codes. Given this traditional

[6]Appadurai (1981: 69) cites A. K. Ramanujam as arguing that *context*-sensitivity is characteristic of Indian social styles as against the *rule*-sensitivity of the European styles.

autonomy of segmental codes, the idea of extensively binding normative orders effective down to particular persons has been relatively alien to India's historical experience. Consequently, India has had difficulty both with *devising* such normative orders as an ongoing process and, more seriously, with *enforcing* them institutionally.[7] Yet it is such general societal codes which allowed Europe to enlarge its operational scales dramatically, and without which a megasociety—especially an industrial megasociety—can count on sinking into very serious difficulties.

As the next chapter will consider, the state in pre-colonial India did occasionally attain considerable size, although in the second millennium these states tended to be organized by ruling groups drawn largely from Central and West Asia. These latter were essentially militarist aristocracies, interested principally in political domination and in the collection of revenues. They lacked both the skills and the stamina requisite for reordering the segmented local universes in another idiom. Symbolic orders associated with these regimes did acquire considerable legitimacy, and one of them could still command attention in 1857; but once the imperial mainspring centred on the emperor ceased to function, as after Aurangzeb's death, the symbolic order by itself could not count for very much. An alternate institutional framework of large scale was lacking, which, appropriating the symbolic order, might give the society autonomous direction. Rather, another *political* mainspring had to be put into position by another empire builder, often from beyond the subcontinent.

The view that the Indian tradition has often operated in a *both/and* logic as against an *either/or* logic ascribed to the West can now be modified. As we have already seen, the European tradition has also been able to accommodate a diversity of purposes, ambitions, and principles; but the difference is that Europe could devise early on what might be called *master codes*: codes which specify authoritatively how the lesser codes, purposes, and so forth may be brought into mutual order. The two early agencies for promulgating such master codes were the Church and the absolutist state.

Among the achievements of the Church we noticed was its effective monopoly over the symbolic order, which was carried to large parts of the population by monks of the mendicant orders—Domi-

[7]Indeed, a move to enforce impersonal norms *institutionally* may readily be branded as being *authoritarian*—or even *fascist*!

nicans and Franciscans—beginning with the 1100s (Duby 1981: 142–6; Erickson 1976: 77–83). The idea of legal codes, in turn, reviving with the 1100s, served absolutist royal power in formulating authoritative legal codes, usable both in administering justice and in bureaucratic functioning (Piltz 1981: 65ff and *passim*). At the royal courts, lying at the centre of the absolutist states, arose too the codes for day-to-day interpersonal courtly conduct. With the arrival of the printing press in the mid-1400s, these codes became generally available, not only for voluntary adherence but also for formal instruction in schools (Elias 1978: 102). The Indian traditions have not commonly promulgated unifying master codes of this sort to deal with their own diversity.

V

While the British bid for the mastery of India became operational over several decades, it drew upon social technologies which had long been in the making in Europe. The key ideas of the specialist army, with firm discipline and unitary command, were applied in European armies between 1550 and 1650 (Anderson 1974: 29); and it made possible the deployment of disciplined force in a way which made the large, centralized territorial state viable. It made possible the French dominance over Europe during the 1500s. It also made possible the later British conquest of India. However, as everyone knows, after the initial conquests, and the responses to 1857 and the like, colonial rule in India was sparing in its use of force. Its authority rested rather on the effectiveness of its bureaucracy—which guaranteed, too, that, should occasion arise, force would be available in its support.

British society in the 1700s admittedly did not have an elaborate bureaucratic system; nor were the ideas behind the bureaucratic structures constructed in India, late in the 1700s, learned from practice traditional to India. There was much trial and error as the arrangements moved from those of traders like Clive, who charged what the traffic would bear, to those of governors like Cornwallis, who sought to advance administrative rectitude. Ad-hoc, small-scale coping invariably made the arrangements over-complex in the vast Indian territories; and this ad hocism alternated with radical simplification, redesigning the system overall. Cornwallis' drive to clean up the administration in the late 1780s

and Macaulay's to codify the laws in the 1830s were such moments
of radical redesigning. These drives rested on explicit general
principles, drawn from the wider European tradition of government, though in a particular case these may be traced to a specific
theorist, as Macaulay's are to Bentham.[8]

All this is sometimes interpreted as part of the colonial ploys,
for advancing the grips of colonialism and capitalism in India.
Debunking in this mode is useful and necessary for keeping issues
in perspective; but thought composed of debunking alone, whatever its worth as polemic, cannot attain to sound judgement.
Macaulay initiated the construction of integrated, impersonal
codes in India. Access to, and the enforcement of, such codes—in
law, and also in bureaucracy and other organizational settings—
is essential to the possibility of any kind of sustained large-scale
operations; it is essential for making megasociety possible.

What this meant for India, then, was that the colonial regime
organized—partly to ensure efficient collection of the tribute which
it thought was its due as a conquering power—the construction
of a large-scale techno-social frame for the subcontinent. This
frame was partly physical, as in the railways; and partly administrative: in the state's monopoly over force and over taxation, and
in the unification first of bureaucratic controls and, second, of the
courts of law. *Given this enlarged, unified frame*, other processes
followed; and social historians have documented these carefully.

For some, there opened career paths of considerable physical
and social range, increasingly routed through institutions of formal,
Western education (illustratively, Conlon 1977). At least in the
colonial capitals, there arose voluntary associations, journals and
other organs of public opinion, joint stock companies, and the
like (Dobbin 1972). And there were new forms for public conduct,
taking their legitimatory ideas from current Western ideologies
and practices, which culminated in the various strands of the
Indian national movement (Mehrotra 1971). Into all this there
certainly flowed, processes traditional to Indian society too
(Conlon 1977; Dobbin 1972; van den Dungen 1968); but the often
ignored, critical fact is that the overall techno-social frame, which
made the beginnings of a megasociety possible, was designed and

[8]On early colonial administration, the *Cambridge History of India*, vol. 5
(Dodwell 1929), especially Chs. 7 to 18, 25, and 26. I thank Sabyasachi
Bhattacharya for this volume. On Macaulay, Stokes (1959: 219–33).

instituted by the colonial regime. Similarly, the models for many
of the subsequent processes also were unambiguously Western in
origin: social mobility without invidious constraints; a public
arena and its voluntary associations; a normative and legal order
to which the colonial state itself was, or could be made to be,
subject; capitalism and mass production; electoral routines for
entry into key political roles; and so forth.

VI

This colonially designed and built techno-social frame was adapted
and expanded considerably after Independence, especially during
the first thirty years. To pick a few indicators at random: the new
Constitution conferred franchise on all adults, expanding the
range of electoral participation dramatically; the general index of
industrial production rose from 73 in 1951 to 256 in 1973; tele-
phone connections rose from 1.11 lakhs in 1947–8 to nearly 13
lakhs in 1973–4; although the community development programme,
initiated in 1951, gave way to *panchayati raj* in the 1960s, and
neither was a spectacular success, administrative linkages directed
at purposes other than revenue collection undoubtedly reached
much deeper into rural society than previously; enrolment of
university students grew from less than 4 lakhs in 1950–1 to over
31 lakhs in 1970–1.[9]

Many felt that the frame and the associated styles were alien to
the Indian tradition; but the latter seemed not to yield much by
way of designs and styles appropriate to a megasociety, except for
terms like panchsheel and panchayati raj. The difficulty in large
part was that the Indian tradition has not had very much by way
of institutions that could be constitutive of a megasociety on a
durable basis. Furthermore, the entrenched local structures of
power and privilege showed an uncanny capacity for capturing
not only the run-of-the-mill institutions like community development projects, but also such alternate initiatives as *bhoodan*,
gramdan, and the like (Ocmmen 1972: Chs. 6 and 7). Willy nilly,
therefore, India has had to work in, and with, a frame to whose
designing and construction it has not been able to contribute

[9]The statements on industrial production, telephones, and rural development follow the papers by Prem Shankar Jha, Yogesh Atal, and T. N. Madan
in Dube (1977); that on university enrolment Kaul (1974, 2, 6).

very much that is hallowed by its ancient traditions.

In the earlier years of independence this frame had a certain momentum; and those working it—including men in politics like Nehru and Patel—took its underlying premises as axiomatic. But these premises included certain implicit assumptions concerning how most actors in the system ought to, and would, behave: assumptions which the passing years have made less and less tenable. To take a well-known early example, Partap Singh Kairon, Chief Minister of Punjab from 1956 to 1964, brought to his office a style which thought nothing of cutting across carefully established routines in achieving his objectives. Kairon's objectives often had a wider social dimension, seeking to arouse grassroots initiative in economic and other activity. His willingness to cut administrative corners led him at times to harrass his officials; and in later years this harrassment of officials was on occasion directed at helping 'his sons or relatives to acquire or dispose of properties or business in violation of law or rules of established procedure'.[10] What had seemed to be aberrations in Nehru's last years became commonplace later.[11] The arbitrary use of power in self-serving ways has virtually ceased to be news; a style which had been introduced by the British in the late 1700s has, over the past three decades, been subject to strong erosive pressures.

Given the coexistence of these two conflicting codes in the milieu, every institution in the land has provided the setting for, and often the reality of, such erosion. The durability and vigour of institutions rest on performances to predictable standards by most actors associated with the institutions; and this is likely to be realized only when related standards and patterns of conduct are being learned extensively—propagated by the same or other institutions, perhaps through routine experiences early in one's life, possibly within the family of one's birth. This happened in the West historically, over the long term, by way of the influence of the Church and its ancillary institutions in the local community

[10]Mangat Rai (1973: 217) citing the Report of the S. R. Das Commission of Inquiry into charges against Kairon. Mangat Rai was Chief Secretary of Punjab under Kairon and provides a generally sympathetic account of Kairon's style.

[11]Prakash Tandon's testimony (1980: Ch. 17) of his relations as Chairman, State Trading Corporation, with L. N. Mishra, his Minister, during the early 1970s is revealing.

(Duby 1981 : 146; Erickson 1976 : 77–83). Comparable magnitudes of influence are not currently available in India: the consequent gaps may be called the *social blanks*. In their place, we have a plethora of codes associated traditionally with the various social segments; and attempts to act these *multiple codes* out in the mega-societal institutions lead to rather different patterns in public conduct. Let us consider these latter first.

VII

We can now distinguish several levels where the multiplicity of codes in contemporary Indian society can be shown to have originated. There was, first, the juxtaposition of the unified code of European extraction (Code E) with the contrastive Indian style of functioning (Code I).[12] There have been, secondly, the variety of segmental codes within Indian society, (Codes I_1, I_2, I_3, . . .), associated with caste-like, normatively insulated social categories, including those bearing distinctive religious traditions. Thirdly, in recent decades Indian society and polity have absorbed diverse other codes—or styles of functioning—too: ideologies of militant protest against oppression and exploitation, real or imagined, in whatever form; patronage and loyalty; reciprocal exchange in network relationships; and so forth. Let us consider each of these levels in some detail.

One aspect of the Code E: Code I interface lay within the colonial bureaucracy. Kaviraj has recently noted that its upper layers had to function 'in a social language that the colonial office understood'; but 'the lower bureaucracy—the enormous administrative underworld too vast and too insignificant to be transformed' directed its discourse to other quarters (1984 : 227). 'Under the thin crust of Europeanised elite, the British had tolerated the untroubled continuance of large expanses of vernacular graft . . . . For each decision there was the internal distance in this large and ill-regulated machine, as it journeyed from adumbration as a policy, through its transmission, decimation and eventual ironical "implementation", often in unrecognisable forms' (ibid. : 232). Post-colonial land reforms are the case Kaviraj cites in point.

[12]In identifying these codes, 'E' may be taken to stand for European, and also for external; 'I' for Indian, but also for internal or integral. Saberwal (1982) offers this theme in an earlier version.

Another aspect of this interface lay in the fact that various groups within India found it possible to spread into an enlarged space formed under the techno-social frame rising under colonial auspices. The spectacular expansion of some merchant castes, including Marwaris (Timberg 1978) and artisan castes, including Ramgarhias (Saberwal 1976), are cases in point. Given the plasticity of a group's internal, multivalent segmental ties, it could in such cases recognize 'opportunity' in the larger space and reorient its internal ties to seize it: an illustration of the 'modernity of tradition' argument. The later mobilization of caste groups, whether to apply pressure publicly, as with the Nadars in the late 1800s and early 1900s (Hardgrave 1969) or to bargain for electoral representation (Rudolph and Rudolph 1967 : 53ff), illustrates too the drive for segmental advance by availing of the larger techno-social frame and its norms and institutions, which had been established by outsiders.

Examined through a sociologist's eyes, the historical landscape displays still other facets of the Code E : Code I interface. These turn on the general proposition that the indigenous society had long had autonomous, segmental spaces; but the self-regulative capacities of these segments were not always wholly adequate, and so the segments often resorted to the institutions of the colonial regime for help in managing their internal affairs. In South Indian temples, we learn from Arjun Appadurai (1981 : Ch. 2), disputes over temple management would have been settled in the Chola or Vijaynagar regimes through 'administrative arbitration' by the ruler or his representative; but this intervention would have been context-sensitive, attentive to the local balance of forces, not much bound by rules or precedents. Called to a similar role of administrative arbitration, the colonial regime balked; and instead it commissioned its courts to constitute a rule-based, elective authority to manage temples' affairs autonomously. This effort rested on premises drawn from European social and political experience; but, given their lack of fit with Indian traditions, it led to considerable imbroglios in the 1800s and the early 1900s—anticipating in good measure the later difficulties of the larger political system in India.

In a variation on this theme, men in a segmental space who seek to reorder it discover that its internal resources and practices do not allow them to be effective. The segmental spaces were autonomous, but the structure of authority internal to them tended to be either ambiguous or lacking in recursive discipline, that is, a discipline which binds its authorities to its own general rules. Christine Dobbin tells us (1972: Chapters 3 & 5) that in the Bombay of the later 1800s several college-educated men undertook to reform their own caste group, seeking to canalize its corporate resources in ways more suitable to the contemporary scene. They found themselves blocked by those wielding traditional authority within the group, authority which was immune to effective challenge within the groups' boundaries. Several of the reformers challenged this authority in the courts of the colonial regime. The courts' decisions tended, on balance, to subvert the authority of the caste heads. The English judge in one famous case declared that 'what is morally wrong cannot be theologically right' (cited in Dobbin 1972: 70), arrogating to himself the right of moral judgement in matters internal to the caste; in another case the court decided that 'the *majority* of the caste had the right to determine in whose custody caste property should be vested' (ibid.: 128; emphasis mine), invoking a general principle which has been important in the Western political tradition.

The Code E : Code I interface had other attributes too. When contemporary practice was seen to violate humanistic norms held to be universal, as with sati, such practices were put down. More steadily, especially until the mid-1800s, colonial courts sought to act on what they could ascertain as authoritative, indigenous law though, given segmentation, this presented difficulties (Rudolph and Rudolph 1967: Pt. 3). On the whole, right until the end of the colonial regime, Code E was acknowledged to be in overall control, constituting the social space within which Codes I_1, I_2, etc. could operate.

During the colonial period, the legitimacy of Code E overall had been questioned principally within contexts of the national movement, though this questioning was *tactical* in the main; for the movement's own efficacy depended heavily on Code E being applied recursively to the exercise of colonial authority itself. As the colonial regime drew to its end, however, pressures began to mount for the use of public power relatively arbitrarily. Lance Brennan, writing of Rohilkhand in Uttar Pradesh, notes that, following the 1937 elections, the Congress government was keen 'to establish its authority over the administration and to demonstrate its ability to rule' (1977: 481). It moved effectively to limit local political pressure on the civil service and to ensure the continuing autonomy of the administrative process. Following the 1946 elections, however, these restraints became weaker, and local politicians began partaking more actively in directing the flow of administratively allocated supplies and other opportunities (ibid., 490–94). Gradually, Code E increasingly came to be seen largely as a decorative element, to be retained until the time was ripe to discard it.

Subsequently, one can discern a style, associated with a group traditionally being displayed by some of its members in megasocietal space; for example, in the early 1980s, the display of a warrior Sikh style under Bhindranwale's impulse. More often, as the constraints associated with the colonial regime gave way, the social and institutional fields appeared to lie open to a great variety of alternate strategies. Illustratively, the various groups, $I_1, I_2, I_3, \ldots$, become substantialized, to use Dumont's word (1970a: Art. 112), competing or coalescing opportunistically in the struggle for resources: thus, the struggles between caste blocks in Karnataka, Bihar, Uttar Pradesh, and elsewhere; between Scheduled Castes and the others (as in Marathawad: Punalekar 1981); and so forth. In other settings, the inherited codes and identities are of little avail; how one acts is not much constrained by a shared sense of right and wrong: anything goes! L.N. Mishra (see n. 11) was a Brahmin, but his political style was scarcely Brahminical in any recognizable sense. Under such conditions, the variety of possibilities in any situation includes amoral opportunism.

Amoral opportunism in the political realm may take such forms as capturing polling booths by force, bribing legislators to switch parties, or harnessing gubernatorial discretion to dismiss a rival ministry. Given a milieu with growing amoral opportunism, socialist rhetoric may camouflage 'an essentially precapitalist alphabet of social action', that is, the use of force and of arbitrary power for private gain (Kaviraj 1984: 234). Others may forge amoral networks or factions for similar gains. With multiple codes espoused in institutional settings, sometimes combatively, it becomes increasingly difficult to mount organized action over the larger space-time wholes, action which depends on widely shared operational codes and definitions of situations. The historic significance of the inherited multiplicity of codes within Indian society, then, is this: it is not that these codes are accurately transferred to mega-societal space, each group or category carrying its custo-mary code; it is rather that there is a general lack of awareness of the crucial importance of unified codes for sustained, large-scale actions. The latter would include action directed at constituting and renewing mega-societal institutions and the corresponding social spaces.

VIII

The multiplicity of codes has another face, long familiar to socio-logists: *anomie*. When actors can feel justified in a great variety of mutually incompatible courses of action, we have a situation lack-ing in social norms, a situation of normlessness. Illustratively, late in 1980, the then Acting Vice Chancellor of Jawaharlal Nehru University expelled a student leader from the University for breach of discipline: the student had gone to the V.C.'s office and abused him in connection with another student's expulsion from a University hostel. The student leader's expulsion evoked a strike by students and prolonged closure of the University. Shortly after these events I overheard another student telling a small group in the lawn that the student leader's expulsion was unjustified: 'If a son goes and abuses his father, will the son be expelled from his home? For the V.C. to be abused is no big thing. There was no good reason for this strong punishment'. Such a familial norm may be current in some corners of Indian Society: but whether it could be stretched into a University today is a question which neither the speaker nor the audience, all members of a university community, seemed able to consider with critical, detached judge-ment. Without such judgement, a multiplicity of codes, that is, anomie, comes to befog institutional life.

From this incident we can move to a more general context. Sociologists use the term 'to institutionalize' at two levels. At one level is *normative support*—the shared sense of approval, of some-thing being right: we say that a course of action, or the principle underlying the course of action, is institutionalized when it has this normative support. At another level, these courses of action, or principles underlying them, may be *reinstitutionalized*: that is, their conduct, their monitoring, or their enforcement may be vested in special, formally designated roles, role-relationships, or role-complexes called institutions. A society's general norms of conduct may thus be put into formal legal codes, and their application entrusted to specially constituted courts of law.[13] Whether or not institutions at this second level have grassroots normative support at the first level would make all the difference to the quality of their functioning.

Needless to say, the institutions of the colonial techno-social frame and its later elaborations have not had very much of this grassroots normative support; for the grassroots normative orders in India, as we have seen, have been quite different from that which generated the rise of institutions in Europe. Between the formal, corporate charters and objectives of these institutions, and the normative pressures operative on persons acting within them, there has, consequently, often been a conspicuous lack of fit. Between these two levels—the formal and the corporate as against the informal and the individual—there is a certain tension everywhere, known to sociologists as the Hawthorne effect (Homans 1950: Ch. 3; Roethlisberger 1977: 46 and *passim*); but in an *anomic* situation, informal, individual, private goals can come to overshadow the corporate functions; and then one can count on very serious difficulties in institutional functioning, which lies at the heart of a megasociety.

We have a paradox here. Individualism is very much a *Western* idea. Why should the pursuit of individual goals and interests presage *institutional* difficulties? To resolve the paradox, we have to recognize *two processes* important to European history. One of these concerns impersonal codes, illustrated in legal codes, bureaucratic manuals, or even in the guides for etiquette[14] and the like. We have noted the centrality of such codes for enlarging the time-space wholes within which much conduct associated with the modern West has come to be located. Put otherwise, the relative impersonality of legal and bureaucratic functioning is central to the modern, large-scale state. Yet there are difficulties in coping with that impersonal universe, in maintaining *personal* meaning *vis-a-vis* the vast impersonal institutional settings. Witness the waves of the young who, 'dropping out' in the West, regularly seek an escape in India.

[13]My formulation here rests on Bohannan's discussion apropos legal codes (1965: 34ff), but the issue applies to a much wider range of institutions.

[14]See Norbert Elias' important *The Civilizing Process* (1978), esp. vol. 1, pp. 101f.

Countervailing this process, however, the West has also sustained a tradition of making the *individual* the locus both of ultimate value and of one's ultimate responsibility for oneself, for constructing one's own meanings, and for directing one's own actions. A much older theme received particularly clear expression in eighteenth-century German philosophy and literature (Taylor 1975: 29–34). Kant's formulation of the categorical imperative posited the rational actor's autonomous reason, able to define courses of action for oneself such that the corresponding principles could be made universal laws too (Scruton 1982: 69–71). That is to say, a rational actor should be able to determine his own course of action by asking whether its consequences would be acceptable even if everyone else were to act the same way. It is through the application of such tests to everyday conduct that an attitude of self-invigilation, to use Kaviraj's term (1984: 235, *passim*), came to exercise its considerable influence in the life of institutions in Western history.

In contrast to the foregoing, as we have seen, the grain of Indian society has run in the direction not of unified, impersonal codes but of multiple, segmental ones, so that Indian tradition has not displayed notable capabilities either for devising unified codes or for promulgating reorganized ones in any considerable social depth. If the relatively impersonal modes of institutional functioning are prerequisites of the satisfactory functioning of modern, large-scale states, then we in India have serious difficulties at both ends: we tend to surrender such institutional norms much too easily to the counter-norms operative in our intimate social milieus; and, at the other end, our traditions do not instil in us, as particular persons, either the norms or the skills which would be needed for accepting ultimate responsibility for oneself and for constituting one's own meanings (see Dumont 1970b).

IX

To sum up, the stability and continuity of traditional Indian society belonged principally to social groupings of small scale: the village, the *jati* and the like. First under colonialism, and then under Nehru and the regime of capitalism, the society was forced-marched into becoming a megasociety; and under Nehru India acquired, too, the ambitions of large-scale co-ordination, connected with the five-year plans and the visions of modernization. Juxtaposed to these

collective ambitions are the individual ambitions, values, and moti-
vations, derived very largely from the cellular world of the family
and the caste—when these are not wholly anomic. The directions
for one's conduct, and interpretations of fresh experience—
even in the mega-societal institutions—are often framed by the
small-scale moralities (Furer-Haimendorf 1967: 117, 225ff) whereby
one's self, kin, or caste-mates come first; though in the recent past,
the identities have come to be associated, at times closely, with
one's linguistic or religious categories too. Dumont (1965: 99,
passim) among others has stressed the importance of the 'holistic'
view in Indian thought; but this whole has in historical experience
tended to be small in scale; and *these* small wholes have in recent
decades been giving way.

We have seen that institutions in contemporary India have
tended to be relatively vulnerable. The older ones from precolonial
times, such as temples or the caste system, can scarcely keep step
with the megasociety, though the resources of a Tirupati may go
into building a college. In the more recent institutions—universities,
bureaucracies, and the like—the calculus of personal advantage
displaces all too often that of corporate purpose, so that we have
at best weakly institutionalized routines for recognizing, and for
pressing, the interests of the collectivity. Visions appropriate to the
larger societal wholes can prevail only if institutions of corresponding scale are deeply entrenched, can defend their own integrity,
and are actively engaged in projecting such visions.

Constructing a megasociety meant a dramatic expansion of the
potential scale of social relationships; but the direction of this
virtually irresistible expansion was set externally. The general
premise in India has been that we can cope with this expansion—
in a way, an expansion of the external world—without affecting
our cultural traditions or the structure of our primary groups, such
as the family or the caste, wherein one's sense-of-the-self is commonly grounded. Taking for granted the versatility of institutions
like the family, we have expected them to provide the social and
psychic support requisite for coping with the changing larger
scene. Millions of people over the decades have, indeed, made
successful day-to-day adjustments; but cumulative, persistent
enlargement of scales generates disturbances which can be met
adequately only through systematic reordering and redesigning
at different social levels.

Physical and social mobility, political participation, industrialization, and similar processes cleave into the older social forms but are powerless to reorder our sense of the self or our modes of social relationships in ways viable over the long run. Such reordering, to make a difference, has to be extensive; and that needs institutional capabilities to match. It takes a shared commitment to form the will to live by reason, to form social bonds open-endedly and to care for them. In this regard we have seen that our heritage has been weak, and the institutions taken from the West have tended too easily to succumb to the urge of personal, private interests. Tensions accumulate consequently at levels both individual—yielding nervous breakdowns—and collective—yielding social breakdowns, as in communal riots. Vivekanand, Tagore, Gandhi and others of their ilk sought to reconstitute our ideas and arrangements at several levels; but the momentum of such initiatives has not been sustained. We live amidst vast changes but without the institutionalized capacities, individual and collective, requisite for meeting the attendant tasks, whose magnitude history has set for us.

CHAPTER III

MEDIEVAL POLITICAL TRADITIONS

How force is deployed, how it is legitimized into the institutions of power and authority, and the resilience and durability of these political institutions—we have suggested that these issues are central to the long-term fortunes of a society. This chapter will review the core ideas, relationships, and institutions which informed three series of medieval Indian polities: in the North, (1) the Rajputs; and (2) the Saltanat[1] and the Mughals; in the South, (3) the Cholas and Vijayanagar. These were relatively durable polities of considerable spatial extent, and between them they cover large parts of the medieval Indian political spectrum. My task is made the easier since all of them have in recent years been considered at length by sociologically sensitive historians. I shall argue that state-building in pre-colonial India remained a cyclical process, subject to the rise and fall of dynasties over relatively brief time spans, whereas the post-Roman states in Western Europe learned to keep steadier course over much longer runs of time. To this learning the Roman Catholic Church contributed decisively.

RAJPUT POLITY

Studies in social structure and social history through much of North India bear witness to the widespread dominance of Rajputs in large parts of this region.[2] This pattern has been noticeable especially in rural areas recently, for Rajput polity has always included a large element of *localized* dominance; but we shall see that this was part of much wider struggles for control during the precolonial period.

---

[1]Sultanat and Sultanate are alternate spellings, but I use the form to which Indian medievalists are switching.

[2]E.g. *Gujarat*: Steed 1955, Shah 1982; *Rajasthan*: Carstairs 1957, Stern 1977, Ziegler 1978; *Madhya Pradesh*: Mayer 1960; *Uttar Pradesh*: Fox 1971, Minturn and Hitchcock 1966; *Himachal*: Parry 1979.

Further back in time, B. D. Chattopadhyaya has documented the gradual constitution of the Rajput category during the late first and early second millennia, out of the families ruling in localities in Gujarat and Rajasthan, and commonly known by such terms as Rajaputras (lit. sons of kings) and its cognates. Marriages between these ruling families were a major device for constituting the caste. Over time the lines of descent received increasing recognition, though the social category has retained an openness to new groups admitted into the Rajput fold 'by virtue of their political initiative and power' (Chattopadhyaya 1976: 77).[3] 'The consolidation of Rajput structure may be viewed', Chattopadhyaya adds cautiously, 'as a result of collaboration between the emerging clans, not only in terms of inter-clan marriage relationship but also in terms of parti-cipation at various levels of polity and the circulation of clan members in different kingdoms and courts' (ibid.: 77). These themes echo through much Rajput experience in later centuries.

Rajput styles of dominance have been supported by socialization for inter-personal aggression (e.g., Steed 1955: 114f and *passim*; Minturn and Hitchcock 1966: 144f and *passim*), and facility with the use of force has undoubtedly served historically to reiterate the domination. The Rajput social frameworks for the exercise of power have been constituted out of two sometimes competing principles: one is kinship, including the ties of both descent and marriage; the other is the tie between patron and client or master and servant. Sometimes an affinal link would follow the line of clientship and, as we shall see, the social boundary within which this could be done has been subject to redefinition in the light of historical circumstances. Interlinked webs of kinship, affinity, and clientship

---

[3]In his study of the structure of caste groups in the Gujarat region, A. M. Shah (1982: 11, *passim*) notices a similar openness of Rajput boundaries to several other dominant groups. Furthermore, whereas other non-Rajput cate-gories of comparable size in Gujarati society are segmented internally, by lines successively of commensality and connubium, the Rajputs in Gujarat are said to have *no* such internal divisions (ibid.: 7, 10). That is to say, they maintain a remarkably open field for sociability and for marriage; and this may have helped historically in political prospecting. Rajputs in village communities elsewhere, however, *are* segmented much like their neighbours (in Western Uttar Pradesh: Minturn and Hitchcock 1966: 31f; near Indore in Madhya Pradesh: Mayer 1960: 154) and the lack of this internal segmentation noticed by Shah may be specific only to some Rajput strata.

helped constitute far-flung social fields accommodating numerous independent rulerships and overseeing the dominance in localities. At least in medieval Rajasthan, the Rajputs came to enforce a virtual monopoly over exercising power, and indeed over competing for it, though this reflected in part their willingness to open Rajput status to new groups emerging to dominance, including immigrant Muslim ruling groups as early as the 1400s (Ziegler 1973: 58–66).

In the formation of Rajput identities in a later medieval period, Norman Ziegler (1978: 223) stresses the weight of the tie between a three-to-six-generational patrilineal group (*khamp*) and a territory over which it claimed hereditary control, although the *khamp* was also part of a much wider patrilineal brotherhood. In some regions, as in western Marwar, ties within the brotherhood remained egalitarian, and the distribution of lineages defined the effective political framework; but elsewhere the brotherhood came to be stratified internally in terms of wealth and access to power and authority which was organized in terms of rulership and clientship. Growth in the size of a state meant growth in ties of the latter sort, for a ruler's authority carried best along these, where expectations of allegiance and loyalty defined the relationship with the client.

Later Rajput polity functioned around a hierarchy of rulerships; the Thakur ruling over a locality, who would submit to the Raja at the regional level, who in turn would acknowledge subordination, by the late 1500s, to the Mughal Emperor. Outside kinship, access to land and positions of authority lay through clientship to a ruler, a multistranded tie which, especially at the local level, would be cemented 'with a vow, sworn before a *devata* (deity) in a local temple' (ibid.: 225). The client would submit to and bear arms for the ruler who would maintain and protect him; and these implications were expressed in several symbolic ways.

Clientship was at times buttressed by ties of affinity: the affinal relationship provided a code in which to make political statements. As in much of North India the wife-taker was culturally defined as being superior to the wife-giver; and a person could acknowledge someone publicly as his master by giving him his sister or daughter in marriage. This would be a statement of political submission and, in this idiom, the tie of affinity became one with that of patron/client; for it was common for a master so acknowledged to provide for his follower or client. Such provision commonly meant a jagir, one or more villages for the allottee, the jagirdar, to rule; and it carried too a commitment of mutual support over the long run. Many castes would live in villages so allotted, including lower ranking Rajputs; but the ranks of jagirdars would have few other than Rajputs.

Whereas during the run up to, and during, the early Saltanat, say the 1100s or even the 1200s, Hindu chieftains often stood aloof, seeming to ignore the Muslim rulers (e.g. Hardy 1978: 207), in later centuries the fact of Muslim power in India came to be gradually accepted (Hardy 1978; Ziegler 1973: 58–66). There was also the learning, on the other side, of the necessity to incorporate indigenous functionaries into the state structure centred in Delhi. During the 1500s, several Rajput rulers suffered numerous defeats at the hands successively of Sher Shah Suri and Akbar (Ziegler 1978: 218f). By then, Rajput ideology had been admitting Muslim warriors, who were rulers too, to Rajput status (Ziegler 1973: 59ff; 1978: 235): this would enable one to treat with the Mughals and the like as one would with other powerful Rajputs. The Rajput political repertoire included the affinal clientship strategy; and several Rajput princesses were married to Mughal royalty (Ziegler 1978: 238f has details).[4]

By the late 1500s, the implications of centralized Mughal power were being felt in Rajasthan. Rajput rajas were fitted into the mansabdari order. Ziegler notes the Mughal preference increasingly for the relatively larger states in Rajasthan (1973: 160–9, *passim*; 1978: 226); and with the assurance of Mughal political support, Jodhpur—the case studied by Ziegler—was able to enlarge its span of territorial control. This made possible an increase in the number of those who would hold lands and villages as clients of the Raja of Jodhpur. Given the example of the Mughal revenue system and the obligations of being a mansabdar (Sharma 1977: 290f), the administrative arrangements in Jodhpur moved towards greater systematization, as with the issue of written titles to land; yet the term 'bureaucratic' can be applied to them (as in Ziegler 1978: 227) only in its looser, less stringent sense.

Rights to land within any particular Thakur domain, the *thikana*, were becoming complicated by the 1600s. In the details examined by Ziegler (1978: 228f) for Bhadrajun *thikana*, a differentiation of

[4]These marriages did violate other parts of the Rajput code of honour, not wholly salved by glossing the Mughals as Rajputs. In the wake of this contradiction, at least one murder followed (see Ziegler 1978: 222f).

rights on varied grounds is noticeable. The choicest lands and villages were held by the ruling family on grounds of birth, and these constituted an inner circle in the *thikana* along with the holdings of the cadet lines of the *khamp*, which were based partly on service to the senior line and partly on rights of birth in the lineage. Around this core was an outer circle of lands and villages allotted to the ruling Thakur's clients from other clans whose only claim to the land was service rendered to the Thakurs; and some clients had given a daughter to the Thakurs too. Some titles to land were written, others informal; some were held individually, others collectively. Some rights, finally, had been secured from the Thakurs, others from the Raja in Jodhpur; and in similar *thikanas* elsewhere, rights could be secured from the Mughal Emperor directly too.

There was thus a multiplicity of forms and ways of acquiring land rights in one *thikana*; and correspondingly there were considerable personal moves physically and a wide range of possibilities open to a Rajput: persisting with the solidarity of one's own kin group or seeking service with the ruler of one's own, or of another clan, or with the Mughal Emperor. During the 1500s and 1600s several Rajputs in Ziegler's cases move conspicuously back and forth between these levels, giving their lives what Ziegler calls a 'disconnected quality' (ibid.: 231). This discontinuity was at times particularly marked in the move to the Mughal Emperor, for there the Rajput value of loyalty to one's master could be in conflict with another Rajput value of not killing a clansmate, for the latter might be necessary in service to the Mughals.

To sum this section up, key elements of the Rajput polity were enmeshed closely with the logics of patrilineal kinship, of affinity, and of personalized clientship. The establishment of Mughal suzerainty over Rajasthan contributed to an enlargement of Rajput states, and this enabled an enlargement of the scales of clientship ties focussed on the Raja of Jodhpur, and possibly some of the other rajas in other parts; and some administrative systematization also followed. In the new context, the Rajputs served the Mughals in other parts of the Empire too, but their own social and institutional resources for state construction were not much augmented. This became evident in the 1700s, for when Mughal control broke down, it was the Marathas who became the arbiters of Rajput fortunes (Ziegler 1973: 4; Sharma 1977: Chs. 9 and 10).

THE SALTANAT AND MUGHALS

If the exercise of power in Rajput kingdoms relied considerably on ties of kinship, affinity, and clientship, and that in successive regimes in Tamil country (considered in the next section) supplemented such ties with integrative devices centred on the temple, statecraft in the series of North Indian Saltanat dynasties (12th–15th centuries) appears to have resorted rather more to heavy applications of force.

The older concept of the *khalifa* had denoted the political head of the state, but it had implied a religious function too. Tenuous though this religious connection had been, it was missing completely from the later conception of the Sultan, who was seen as a temporal sovereign alone. Though it was an old Arabic word, 'Sultan' picked up associations from the Iranian imperial tradition and, by the eleventh century, it came to denote secular rulership, with Mahmud of Ghazni (1000–1030) recognized as the first Sultan. Released from the fluctuating constraints of Islamic law, the shariat, legitimate power now came to be concentrated in the hands of the ruler, the Sultan, to the point where, 'it was the ability of the Sultan to destroy and reward—that set him up over and above his fellow beings. That was all'. (Athar Ali 1982 relying upon Barani the fourteenth-century historian.)

The men who left their mark on the Saltanat—Balban (1266–86), Alauddin Khilji (1296–1316), Muhmmad Tughlaq (1325–51)—are commonly known for their capacity to subjugate adversaries by force, and in being able to do so peremptorily, brooking no opposition[5] (Athar Ali 1982; M. Habib 1981: 148–270 and elsewhere). Religious fervour would continue to be aroused in later warfare, but in Sultanship there was no longer a religious connection to help legitimize a ruler as such. These Saltanat regimes are remarkably sanguinary (e.g. M. Habib 1981: 364, 387) echoing patterns common then to Central Asia (see S.M. Ikram 1964: 30f), including Turkestan, the area of origin of most rulers of the Saltanat.

[5]Dr Muzaffar Alam has reminded me that the very Sultans known for their ruthless use of force are known too for their measures to systematize administration in the Saltanat with regard to constructing irrigation canals, collecting revenue and related tasks.

Extraordinary bursts of conquering activity that covered very large parts of the subcontinent marked the Saltanat. Numerous, mutually unrelated immigrants from Central and West Asia contributed to this vigour. Some of them were brought in as part of a widespread system common to medieval Islamic states in West Asia, wherein a ruler would buy highly valued 'slaves' coming from foreign lands, who would be wholly at his command, and who would man his army and his administration (M. Habib 1974: 101; 1981: 385)[6]. Deploying these ambitious immigrants, the Saltanat states could triumph, Mohammad Habib has suggested (1974: 20), partly because the indigenes were segmented too severely to be able to combine adequately in their own defence.

The ruler forcing his way—this was central to the conception of the Sultan, and to the practice recurrent under the Saltanat. In this regime, the use of force legitimized itself by success in a venture, and so the more powerful functionaries, even if royal 'slaves' by designation, were often prone to rebel (ibid.: 106, 154f; M. Habib 1981: 360), at times with support from the *ulema* with their extensive social contacts. Even though the Sultan was dependent on his established leading men, the fear that they might be inclined to rebel repeatedly persuaded Sultans to decimate large numbers of potential challengers, their senior functionaries (e.g. Ibn Hasan 1936: 45; M. Habib 1974: 107–10; 1981: 323–34). This was not conducive to stable administrative arrangements over large areas, nor to sound, long-term practice; and though there was a great deal of activity concerned particularly with collecting land revenue, the state structure, especially away from the capital, was often not very firm.

How far this model of the Sultan remained to influence Mughal conceptions of statecraft is a matter for consideration. It may be that, as Iqtidar Alam Khan argues, *the structure of political relationships* fashioned by the Mughals 'drew heavily on the traditions and practice evolved under Turkish rulers [in the Saltanat] of the 13th and 14th century' (1972: 18); while the *ideology* claiming transcendental legitimacy for the Emperor had a wider catchment. In *Akbar-Nama*, Abul Fazl, Akbar's principal ideologue resorted to an ancient origin myth of the Mongols: going back to Adam, he invoked the charisma of a line which counted

---

[6]Richards (1978a: 271f) notes the continuation of the idiom, and of at least some of the associated practice into the 1600s.

both Changhez Khan and Timur, and proclaimed this line to be the carrier of a divine luminosity flowing through the generations to Akbar, conferring upon him 'the enhanced awareness' that made him the 'Master of the Age' (J.F. Richards 1978a: 266). Richards sees Abul Fazl as merging ideas from the 'illuminationist theosophy' of a Persian philosopher, Suhrawardi Maqtul (d. 1191) with the origin myth of the Mongols (1978a: 265f). To these illuminationist ideas, as we shall see below, Akbar would anchor an imperial discipleship.

This legitimizing myth served a structure of power built around Akbar's major efforts in the late 1500s to constitute the mansabdari, the imperial corps which filled key leadership roles in the army and the administration. Athar Ali (1968: 7) notes references to a total of some 8,000 men in this corps, probably *before* the additions late in Aurangzeb's reign; M.N. Pearson (1976: 224), with a more stringent criterion, pares it down to 'about 1,000 men' in the 'core nobility of Mughal India' identified by Richards (1976: 243) as 'provincial governors and *diwans*, field and fortress commanders, *faujdars, amins*, and other officers posted throughout the provinces of the empire'. Richards has examined how these mansabdars were brought into ties of considerable emotional intensity with the Emperor (1976: 242ff; 1978a: 267ff). The state structure arising in the consequent framework of relationships remained invincible for over a century, at least until Aurangzeb's troubles with Shivaji began in the 1660s (Pearson 1976).

Most mansabdars as well as the Emperor were descendants of warrior lineages, sharing the values of 'strength, hardihood, loyalty, and courage' (Richards 1976: 243), and these underlay the corps' 'military ethic'. Promotion in service, and substantial rewards besides, followed upon success in warfare, thus renewing and reinforcing these values (though performances in battle in the empire's declining years were often far from satisfactory: Pearson 1976; Richards 1976). Into this context of shared values Akbar introduced the tie of imperial discipleship which would establish a personal link between the Emperor and the noble-made-disciple:

At noon on Sunday, the Emperor himself presiding, the newly selected disciples underwent an initiation ceremony (in groups of twelve). Each Muslim initiate signed a declaration repudiatin g the orthodox bonds of conventional Islam and agreeing to reverence Allah directly. He also swore to accept four degrees of devotion; the unhesitating willingness to sacrifice one's life, property, religion, and honor in the service of the Master (Akbar). During the ceremony the new disciple placed his head at the feet of the Emperor in the fashion of the Sufi disciple's prostration to his master or Pir. Upon conclusion of the ceremony, the Emperor raised up the supplicant and, placing a new turban upon his head, gave him a symbolic representation of the Sun, and a tiny portrait of Akbar to wear upon his turban (Richards 1978a: 268, proceeding from S.A.A. Rizvi's work).

Given the ethnic and religious diversity of the men drawn into Akbar's service, this personal commitment would serve to tie members of the new Mughal elite individually to the person of the Emperor. The institution appears to have been continued at least by Jahangir who may have reduced it to a much smaller scale, possibly under pressure from Islamic orthodoxy in India (see p. 45 below) (Richards 1987a: 268f).[7]

Only a fraction of mansabdars appear to have entered this discipleship; yet, when in town, members of the corps had to attend the Emperor's court daily in person:

At any audience, the Emperor would be likely to know the record of service; the family, caste, or lineage; the factional and personal affiliation; and the administrative and military qualities of the man standing before him. The process of personal interaction continued at a distance. Those *mansabdars* posted away from the court frequently sent petitions and memorials directly to the Emperor. In an interesting substitute for a personal exchange, these petitions and the Emperor's replies were often read out in public audiences. The Emperor also sent written orders and queries directly to members of his nobility (Richards 1976: 243).

Sons of this military aristocracy expected to follow in their fathers' footsteps as a matter of course. Indigenous groups—Rajput, Khatri, Kayasth, Brahman—also entered the corps on terms they found honourable, at least until Aurangzeb's later years.

Akbar's campaign to focus the symbolism of empire on the Emperor's person (Richards 1978a: 253–9) was all too successful.

[7]For late 1600s, Richards notes Aurangzeb's inability to bring local warrior aristocracies in the Deccan and in South India into the framework of his *close personal relationships*, and the contribution this lack of integration may have made to the troubles of the empire (1976: 245f).

Mansabdars' individual fortunes were to remain dependent upon the Emperor's personal goodwill until the end of the seventeenth century; and this dependence was virtually complete for officials who were first-generation immigrants from Central and West Asia. For them, losing royal favour could mean destitution (e.g., Mukhia 1976: 102ff on Badauni). To cope with such uncertainty, there was much jockeying for royal favours to oneself and one's close kin (Rizvi 1975: 93–123; Richards 1978a: 275), while officials of indigenous descent sought to secure rights in political domains outside *direct* imperial control (Perlin 1981: 280f). This could make for conflicts of interest—part of the centrifugal pulls active in the imperial service already. The sense of insecurity and mutual distrust between the Emperor and his nobles, which had marked the Saltanat, would haunt the 1700s again.

Compared with Christianity in Western Europe in the middle ages, Islam lacked an organized church which might act as an autonomous, and occasionally rival, centre of power, and the *ulema*, remained heavily dependent on the monarch's goodwill. Under the Saltanat they had nevertheless often provided the emotive push to uprisings against the monarch. S. Nurul Hasan (1943) finds here the reason for Akbar's attempts to neutralize the *ulema*, shaping a secular idiom for the symbols of empire to be focussed on the Emperor. His success was partial; witness the strength of the Naqshbandi reaction, forming late in his reign and gaining strength under Jahangir, seeking to reiterate the primacy of orthodox Islam (Aziz Ahmad 1964: Ch. 7; Friedmann 1971).

During the more creative phases of the Saltanat and the Mughals, there was considerable administrative activity, especially concerning revenue extraction and maintaining peace within the regime's domains (Perlin 1981: 283ff has a recent review); but it remained dependent upon assurance over the Emperor's person. The consequences of this dependence were made evident in the immobilization of the regime in periods either of the Emperor's incapacitation, as towards the end of Shah Jahan's reign (Ibn Hasan 1936: 355), or of the struggles of succession, as at the beginning and the end of Aurangzeb's reign (Pearson 1976: 234; Richards 1976: 253).

Under Akbar there are some signs of officialdom beginning to look like a Weberian bureaucracy (M. Athar Ali 1978; Hardy 1976: 261): a firmer differentiation and systematization of functions in the state, and cash salaries for officials. A strong social tug pulled the other way, however: a tug expressed in a general preference for jagirs over cash salaries, with nobles pressing the Emperor—successfully by the early 1700s—to revoke the transferability clause for jagirs in favour of their permanent endowment (for Golconda, Richards 1976: 241; Muzaffar Alam, personal communication); in mansabdari's virtually exclusive focus on the Emperor, without becoming an internal hierarchy where authoritative commands would issue from generalized roles at an administrative centre; and in a corresponding lack of impersonal, generalized codes for the whole gamut of situations, succession to Emperorship onwards. Such criteria for appraising the Mughal regime arise, of course, from the nature of bureaucracies in Europe, but it will be evident that such institutions draw upon styles and resources shaped in a particular context in long historical runs; and these, we have seen, have been very different in India as against Europe.

It would not be correct to say that the Saltanat and Mughal regimes were altogether lacking in general laws. To be sure, much was enclosed within kin, village, and other corporate groups, their relationships regulated in terms of their internal norms and procedures, without recourse to the State's legal arrangements (Ibn Hasan 1936: 339f). Residually, the *kazi* no doubt administered a general law, but its provisions were bounded primarily by the Koran and, where its contents were unavailing, by traditions concerning the Prophet's sayings and actions in his life (*hadith*). The Koran and the Prophet's sayings and actions had referred to a setting rather remote from that of medieval India; yet, given their sanctity, there were limits both to the innovations this sacred law would permit and to the secular systematization it admitted.

There was also the secular law, arising in royal pronouncements and sanctioned by rulership. Its response to the times was unconstrained by sacred traditions, but it expressed the royal will relatively directly (M. Habib 1981: 312ff), without mediation by a cumulative, long-term tradition of general principles in specialists' hands. There were moves towards systematization in revenue administration and in the conduct of official business at least at the centre of the Empire (Ibn Hasan 1936: 353f); but these developments lacked the imprint of a secular legal tradition, such as Europe commanded extensively from the 1100s onwards (Piltz 1981: 65f; see pp. 13f above). As we saw, the Roman legal tradition was revived, initially at the secular schools and universities being founded in Italian cities; and legists trained in the secular techniques of that tradition were drawn into simplifying, systematizing, and generalizing the laws of the several states taking shape in Europe (Bloch 1961: 116–20). This generalizing legal tradition was an important resource in the rise of the absolutist states of subsequent centuries (Anderson 1974: 24–29). The Mughal state did not have access to concepts and skills of this order.

SOUTH INDIA

The medieval south Indian polities are marked by much greater complexities than those associated with the Rajputs and the Mughals, but a series of interconnecting, sociologically informed accounts and reappraisals, coming recently from a group of scholars led by Burton Stein and Arjun Appadurai, clarify as well as redefine the field. The following review is based on this important body of work. These are complex discussions of complex societies changing over long time-spans; and if the discourse is simplified apparently to the point of stereotyping, some compensation may lie in a few major themes coming into clear relief.

There are, to start with, three major political complexes to locate in time and space. First the Pallavas, beginning possibly early in the first millennium A.D. (Dirks 1976: 129f), reviving in the late 600s and reaching a peak with Nandivarman II (c. 731–796), whose kingdom was centred in Tondaimandalam, around the Penner-Ponnaiyar river, discharging into the ocean just south of Pondicherry (Dirks 1976). In the ninth century, the centre of power begins shifting south to the Cholas in Thanjavur in the Kaveri delta. Chola power and influence peak between the 900s and 1100s, reaching west and north, well into Telugu country. In the mid-1300s, Vijayanagar comes into view, initially around the Tungabhadra river in Telugu country in the middle of the peninsula, and for the next three centuries its warriors dominate the Telugu, Kannada, and Tamil areas to the south.

Despite the long time-span at issue, in these regimes the relations of authority, the key institutions, and the associated myths and activities are marked with interlinked transformations of remarkable continuity, such as to permit their consideration together. The key puzzle in these kingdoms is this: both the Cholas and Vijayanagar give suggestions of vast capabilities in their monumental temples and in the large territories acknowledging their overlordship; yet when the Vijayanagar warriors began to move south in the 1400s, they encountered little resistance from the prior regimes. Subsequently, these warriors' principal struggles were not with the peoples over whom they ruled, but with the Vijayanagar kings in whose names they had initially moved (Stein 1980: 370, 409 *passim*). Stein's explanation lies in showing that these were not bureaucratically governed polities but rather:

(1) that the kingdom's Centre, especially for the Cholas, drew the agricultural surplus from the fertile Kaveri delta, supplementing it with predatory raids on distant lands (see below);

(2) that much of this surplus went into endowing *brahmadeyas* and constructing monumental temples, the ritual centres of the regime and core institutions of the society; and

(3) that the differential in organizational capacities between the kingdom and distant localities was not such that the former might enforce imperative co-ordination on the latter in the manner of a bureaucratically organized state. Rather, the localities sought, at their own initiatives, to try to reproduce the prestigious forms of conduct and relationships descried at the ritual Centre—thus showing allegiance to it—but retained an essential autonomy in the disposal of resources as a segment. Hence Stein's label for the regime: a segmentary state.

In the management of power in these regimes, a variety of resources was engaged. Recent analyses have stressed the weight of religious institutions, yet the importance of military prowess for securing resources and establishing dominance in the region is a constant over time (Dirks 1976: 153f for the Pallavas; Stein 1980: 40f, 49 for the Cholas and 400–4 for Vijayanagar). The amount of force deployed jumped sharply with Vijayanagar, whose warriors learned the use of good horses from Deccani Muslims, of artillery from the Portuguese, and of fortification from practices to the north; yet, while its warriors used these to instal themselves over a vast territory, the relations between the Vijayanagar kings and their warriors remained fragile, with the latter pulling continually, and successfully, to go their own way.

In contrast to the Rajputs, the South Indian polities did not make much use of kinship ties in the management of power. While the Rajput ideas on marriage allowed for a wide dispersal of marital ties, recognizing these as an appropriate medium for making statements of political alliance between the families so connected, South Indian kinship has preferred marriage with a cross-cousin or a sister's daughter, tending to renew affinal ties between previously related families. This led to what Stein (1980: 102) has called the 'spatially compressing character of the marriage system' in South India. Ties of clientship, which loomed so large in the later Rajput state, were mediated in South India by the institutional setting of the temple; and it is to a consideration of such institutions that we now turn.

Already, under the Pallavas late in the first millennium, before the shift of power to the Cholas, the political relations are seen to be embedded intimately with ritual ones. Dirks (1976) reviews the successive, wide-ranging transformations in mythology, in relations of authority, and in the form and content of ritual activity since *before* the beginning of the Pallavas early in the millennium. Vedic sacrifices had loomed large in the earlier period. In heightening the identification between the king performing the sacrifice (and his descendants), his key functionaries, and his territory, these rituals for prosperity were seen to advance the welfare of both the king and his kingdom (Dirks 1976: 134–9). In later centuries—late Pallava, Chola—the 'sacrifice' increasingly took the form of giving gifts for sustaining the settlements of Brahmins, *brahmadeyas*, and establishing temples.

The Pallava sovereignty myth was claiming divine origin for them by the late 600s (Dirks 1976: 144), and by the next century the Pallavas were proclaiming their descent from Lord Vishnu. In the emerging ideology, a royal gift 'became an emanation of sovereignty, in which the endowed institution or individual(s) (temple or *brahmadeya*) became actualized expressions of sovereignty, and in that sense made equivalent in ritual terms to the king' (Dirks 1976: 145f).

The *brahmadeyas* were communities of Brahmins upon whom a share in the produce of specified agricultural land had been conferred. Initiated by the Pallava kings, the endowment would enable the Brahmins to cultivate Sanskrit and other religious learning, to transmit it to other Brahmins, and to render certain services of religious significance (Stein 1980: 152). Only the irrigated, fertile tracts could produce the surplus to sustain such specialist communities, and Stein's map (facing p. 150) shows their concentration along river banks, the densest being in the Chola core area in the Kaveri delta. We note in passing that the Brahmins' ritual preferences would also accord with this proximity to flowing water.

Some of these communities were among the largest settlements of their time, and they were notable for their ability to manage their complex affairs autonomously, without external control. It was in their midst that the tradition of sacred chants to Vishnu and Shiva took shape, a tradition which prepared the ground for the later burst of temple-building to these gods,[8] initially of small temples and, beginning with the tenth century, the monumental ones sponsored by the Cholas. Brahmins continued to conduct temple ceremonials, especially in the Kaveri delta and other core areas, thus partaking of the temple resources too; yet the focus of these endowments was no longer the autonomous Brahmin communities but the temple deity, posited to be the sovereign presiding over the temple. Resources would thus be drawn away from the *brahmadeya* communities, generating pressures by the twelfth century which would contribute to their decline subsequently (Stein 1980: Ch. 7; also pp. 156f).

Endowing a *brahmadeya* or a temple had been a privilege open only to members of the royal family, but, by the middle of the eighth century, others unrelated to the royal family, whom Dirks (1976: 151) sees as 'chiefs' in their regions, were being admitted into the royal rituals of endowment, thus partaking of the king's sovereignty themselves, 'entering relations with the central king ... highly valued and mutually advantageous' (1976: 156). Dirks sees these chiefs as a new level of authority, mediating between the king and peasant community, emerging in the course of spreading Pallava influence and the associated expansion of the political system (1976: 152). In subsequent centuries, the privilege of making endowments became much more widely exercised and in Stein's judgement (1980: Ch. 4; also pp. 229f), the vast bulk of endowments for *brahmadeyas* and at least the lesser temples began to originate with dominant peasant groups.

The founding of a temple was seen as generating prosperity, just as the construction of a dam or canal would: and following A. M. Hocart, Dirks stresses the equivalence in underlying thought between temples and reservoirs. In a society rather thin in administrative resources, it was the social arrangements around the

[8]Stein (1980: Ch. 2) locates the impulse for this development in the wide-ranging conflict of preceding centuries, known to South Indian history as the 'Kalabhra interregnum'.

temple that managed the irrigation facilities too (Dirks 1976: 145f; 152); and this would reinforce the association of the temple with prosperity.

In this elaborate ideology, the cycle of rituals and the transactions which evolved around the deity in a temple, a worshipper making an endowment would require the regular provision of certain foods and services to the deity during one or other ritual; and this entitled the worshipper both to participate in the ritual in a prescribed manner, which was an 'honour', and to receive the donor's share of the offering, which had now become *prasadam*, a gift from the deity. In the culture surrounding the temples access to these honours and consecrated foods came to be highly valued entitlements. Numerous complex rituals could be situated in the daily, monthly, and annual calendars of any particular temple,[9] enabling correspondingly numerous donors and others to participate in this dense sequence of activities and flow of honours. Participating recurrently thus both expressed and renewed the devotees' commitment to the ideology underlying the temple overall.

In this ideology the king and deity were seen as being both homologous and in active relationships of mutual support. The deity was sovereign in the temple, as the king was in the palace. Temple and palace were both redistributive centres, exalted, benevolent, receivers of offerings and services, and givers of gifts and honours. The king bestowed resources upon the deity and, as we shall see, 'protected' the orderly conduct of proceedings in the temple; the deity bestowed valued honours on the king. These ritual statements are expressive not only of the deity partaking of sovereignty but also of the king partaking of divinity. The basic logic took shape under the Pallavas, was adopted and expanded dramatically under the Cholas and, as we shall see, it provided room for advancing Vijayanagar purposes too.

The later Chola and Vijayanagar periods witnessed marked expansion in these arrangements: the number of temples grew,[10] more varied groups of worshippers were able to make endowments

---

[9]Appadurai's (1981: 28–32) contemporary calendar for one month, for one large temple in Madras city, provides a measure of the temples' capacities for concerting social participation.

[10]Stein (1977: 12) cites the 1961 Census enumeration of temples constructed between 1300 and 1750 in Tamil country. The number is 10,542.

for the deity and were entitled to specified honours in return, and the rituals accommodating these transactions increased in number and complexity. A donor could confer the donor's quota of foods and honours on his nominees, thus securing the allegiance of the latter. As the complexity of the arrangements involving worshippers, priests, and temple managers grew, disputes between them became more likely; but there was no authoritative control over these relationships (Appadurai 1981: 51), they were often unable to resolve their disputes internally. Yet their expeditious resolution was essential for the orderly conduct of numerous temple rites and their attendant transactions; and to this end, the king or his representative had to intervene.

Appadurai has examined the processes for resolving conflicts concerning temples (1981: Chap. 2) and concludes that the king or his representative sought essentially to encourage reasonable local agreements to be reached and then to make these authoritative. He would *not* turn to general, impersonal codes for the terms on which to settle the particular dispute; the framing of such general codes was not part of the political process. Rather than being *rule-sensitive* in this manner, the prevailing style was *context-sensitive* which Appadurai cites A.K. Ramanujam as holding to be characteristic of the Indian styles generally (1981: 69). Nor did one settlement become a firm precedent for later ones: this would have required the conscious generalization of underlying principles, which would have been out of character. The political style did not seek general principles out of particular experience; it sought, rather, to provide what Appadurai calls administrative arbitration. This royal contribution to the resolution of disputes was highly valued and, as it enabled the temple to function in a relatively orderly way, it was seen as the 'protection' of a temple by the king.[11] These acts were seen to be even more important than the making of fresh donations; and they were part of the mutuality of interests which was thought to tie king and deity together.

Appadurai (1981: 64ff) and Stein (1980: 430ff, 468ff) agree that

[11]When this royal function ended with the establishment of Company rule in Madras, a reluctant colonial state was forced—on pain of disorder—to intervene and to devise alternate arrangements. Given the lack of fit between the two cultural styles in encounter, this latter task proved far trickier than could have been anticipated (Appadurai 1981: Chs. 3–5).

the Vijayanagar rulers and warriors were able to extend and institutionalize their influence in their conquered territories partly by way of the chinks in the temples. They would endow a temple with revenue from numerous conquered villages, directing the donor's share from the deity to the leader of a sect active at the temple whom they made their agent. The agent, in turn, could augment his following by allocating this donor's share to the latter and by using his position in the temple to direct varied resources and honours towards his followers. Between a sectarian leader, able to establish ascendancy within temple affairs, and a Vijayanagar ruler or warrior there could arise a symbiotic relationship exemplified rather spectacularly by the late fifteenth-century figure of Kantatai Ramanuja Aiyankar, who having demonstrated his skills at the Tirupati temple, went on to the temple at Srirangam as the agent of the Vijayanagar ruler as well as, later, of his general in the area (Appadurai 1981: 89f, 94ff).

Such representatives of rulers in the Vijayanagar period did intervene in the affairs of temples, core institutions of the society, but, as we noted, the interventions were essentially *ad hoc*, not in terms of general codes of uniform applicability. This latter, as we have seen, has been a rather particular historic achievement of the West. Even lacking such codes, however, we have noticed the establishment of political fields of relatively large scale in medieval South India. The Chola polity managed to send armies on distant expeditions, to organize irrigation works, and to construct temples on a monumental scale. Chiefs in the localities arose on the strength of the area's dominant peasant castes. They could add their contingents to the Chola raiding expeditions, but their political control in their localities was autonomous; and in their separate localities in the fifteenth century and later, they could find few answers to the superior strength of the Vijayanagar warriors.

The Vijayanagar warriors in turn could, on the strength of superior force, move in and establish their dominance in the several regions. Finding it difficult to control them, the Vijayanagar rulers established a regime of royal fortresses, led by Brahmin army commanders believed to be lacking in independent political ambition on their own account (Stein 1980: 412 *passim*); but this arrangement could not compensate for the lack of a tradition of bureaucratic control and discipline which would make the warriors reliably responsive to the will of the political centre (ibid.: 409 *passim*).

Ties of patrilineal kinship, of affinity, and of clientship had provided the core for the congeries of polities in medieval Rajasthan. As part of the Mughal political system, some of these enlarged the scale of their rulerships, alongside a strengthening of their ties of clientship. A certain formalization of administrative practices followed, but the general Rajput style remained highly personalized in content, though sustaining the shared Rajput sense of dominance over the region.

While marriages were comparatively unimportant for political connections in South Indian polities, the Centre and the localities appear to have been interlinked in several ways: the mobility of Brahmins between localities and of architectural and ritual forms between temples; the ritual incorporation of chiefs into the sovereignty of the royal centre and the co-operation between the king and chiefs in predatory activity; and the king's agent with varied functions around the temple—managing the royal endowments, advancing the patron's political interests, and overseeing the conduct of temple activity on behalf of the king. All this bespeaks rather more interlinking than the plain model of the segmentary state can admit, though Stein is right in holding that such relationships cannot be called a 'bureaucracy' in the strict sense.

At its peak, the Mughal state was the predominant political entity in the subcontinent, surpassing all others. The integration of its more important functionaries into a relatively unified order with a shared militaristic ethic, under Akbar, took it part way to the 'bureaucratic' model; but this *tour de force* was rather fragile. There came a strong reaction to Akbar's attempt to draw his officials away from Islamic orthodoxy into more secular ways (see p. 45), and the pull of local ties was felt over time not only by Rajputs and Marathas but by the immigrant Muslim groups too. That is why Athar Ali's list of traits said to qualify the Mughal Empire as 'a primitive version of the modern state' (1978: 38) remains unconvincing.

Overall, then, organized officialdom was virtually missing in Rajasthan (except later under Mughal tutelage) and in south

Indian polities. It was more salient in the Mughal state, suggesting the seeds of a bureaucracy in the strict sense of the term though, by the later 1600s, its parochializing tendency had become strong. The functioning of the Mughal state depended very heavily upon the ruling dynasty, a dependence which would inevitably have exposed it over the long run to the vagaries of biology (see p. 56f below). In the short run, the Mughal state as well as its immediate predecessors, lacking in firm rules for succession, witnessed debilitating struggles over the issue. Overall, therefore, the political domain in India remained host to cyclical processes of the rise and fall of dynasties, and often it took only a few brief generations to complete the cycle.

During periods of dynastic decline, a region lay open to political adventurers. In North India, more often than not, these adventurers tended to come from Central and West Asia. In earlier centuries the immigrants had settled into the caste order more or less comfortably. Beginning with the Arab conquerors of Sind in the 700s, however, the contrasts between two religious great traditions began to interfere with this assimilability. An antagonistic religious interface would henceforth add to the prevailing segmentation of society; though at times the cleavages would be relieved marginally by administrative and other secondary relationships such as those established by Akbar across the religious interface (see p. 74).

Lack of firm routines for succession, and therefore the recurrent struggles for succession, had weakened the Roman Empire too; and even the most notable of its successor states—Merovingians (c. AD 500–751) and Carolingians (AD 751–987)—were at best only modestly durable. For the cyclical processes of the rise and fall of dynasties in India, one can locate isomorphs here. If European political history took a strikingly different course later, a major part of the explanation lies in the Roman Catholic Church, whose role was discussed in the previous chapter. Briefly, it was largely the Church that enabled Western Europe to grow out of cyclical political processes into others, facilitating the endogenic evolution of *political* and other institutions over the long term. Illustrative of the manifold functions of the Church was that of dissolving such migrants as the German tribes and the Vikings into host populations; and also its capacity to provide political insurance to societies which were then learning, or re-learning, the skills of state construction. When these skills faltered, the Church, heir also to the Graeco-Roman visions of large-scale social order, could provide a major steadying influence. It is appropriate, then, to give this extraordinary institution another brief look in the present context.

The Church was a large institution: already in the 500s, Italy alone had many hundreds of clergymen, managing Church properties, conducting Church offices and correspondence, executing the Pope's will, organizing charity for the poor, performing priestly functions, and so on (Jeffrey Richards 1979: Ch. 17). Subsequent centuries saw a mushrooming of monasteries in addition to these. The senate and the clergy in Rome elected the Pope collegially (ibid.: Ch. 14). Succession to the Papacy was not tied to genealogical links. There were phases when the Papacy tended to go to men who were very old and would last only a brief while (ibid.: Ch. 15, for the fifth to eighth centuries) or who fitted into a mosaic of small time Italian rulers (Holmes 1975: 282–301 and Mallett 1971 for the fifteenth century); yet, repeatedly and especially in moments of crisis, it was men of outstanding competence whom the Church could elect to the Papacy and other high offices. Working in the Church and its ancillary institutions, Popes, bishops, abbots of monasteries and the like were actively engaged not only in sustaining a normative order but also recurrently in the political management of their societies (J. Richards 1979; Duby 1980). This latter tradition and capability became singularly important when kingships tended to falter.

As part of this political management, the Church sought out potentially effective kings and emperors, advised them on the tasks appropriate to rulership, anointed them, thus legitimizing their rule, and provided some constraints on the use of force, thus legitimizing power. These processes were especially important until the states gained the secular resources needed for their own durability and autonomous strength: the rule of primogeniture for succession (Bloch 1961: 189, 203ff, 384–88; Reynolds 1984: 261, 303f); and, later, from the 1200s on, the legal codes articulating an impersonal and systematized normative order, and the bureaucratic frame, manned by university men and engaged in administering the societies. This bureaucracy would function relatively steadily, partly neutralizing some of the biological uncertainties necessarily associated with the rule of succession by primogeniture. As the sources of uncertainty came gradually under control, and the institutions of the state for orderly functioning became entrenched, several parts of Western Europe were able to steady themselves out of the dynastic uncertainties: and the region was spared overwhelming armed invasions by outsiders too. Seen alongside the other thrusts of the period—part institutional, part technological (see Ch. 2)—rather unusual processes of political and related evolution come into view. The long term, more or less cumulative course of these processes, would culminate in the political and economic revolutions of subsequent centuries.

Seen comparatively, then, it is evident that the endowment of medieval India in cultural resources and institutional arrangements left a good deal to be desired by way of materials useable in constructing resilient and durable state structures. Institutions designed after Western prototypes and implanted in the modern period are not layered deep in the Indian tradition. One should not take it for granted that the elements needed to sustain institutions of Western design would ordinarily be available to those located in every part of the Indian social and cultural milieu; and when persons formed in the less helpful of those milieus have to operate and, more generally, cope with these institutions, difficulties of some seriousness may reasonably be expected to arise. Political actors in contemporary India are heirs, on the contrary, to a variety of political traditions coming down from the precolonial period, which makes for a multiplicity of codes in the political arena. Such multiplicity is, in principle, amenable to reduction through analysis, reintegration of ideas, and the restructuring of society; but the requisite skills and institutions are, in turn, not deeply layered. Such multiplicity of codes, it was argued earlier, tends to exact a heavy price.

CHAPTER IV

ELEMENTS OF COMMUNALISM

P.C. Joshi (1980: 168) observes that 'the study of communalism from a macro-sociological or political-economic standpoint has not yet emerged as an important field of enquiry in social science research', and goes on to say that 'very rarely does one come across an attempt to evolve a comprehensive and integrated approach to the problem'. While sharing this judgement in the main, I have come to believe that the phenomenon of communalism can be understood only through an analytic field which acknowledges its multiple levels and whose terms can cope with situations as diverse as, say, the pressure upon Muslims in a village in Mysore (Epstein 1962: 32f) as well as what the historians of medieval India recognize as the Naqshbandi reaction: a movement away from Akbar's search for bridges, doctrinal and political, between Hindus and Muslims (A. Ahmad 1964: Ch. 7; Friedmann 1971). Consequently, when Professor Joshi states that the paucity of work on communalism 'has originated both from a lack of adequate theoretical perspective and of poverty of authentic empirical material', I am rather uneasy; for 'authentic empirical material', often in its wide-ranging context, is strewn through virtually every monograph on Indian society and history, waiting merely for an 'adequate theoretical perspective' to draw it together.

This essay seeks such a perspective. It begins with a synoptic review of the work of sociologists and historians and asks why we have not been able to sustain an interest in communalism. Later it sketches the terms proposed for the analytic field. Material interests are part of this field, and these are especially important in explaining the phenomenon at local, and sometimes regional, levels. These enter the wider processes too, but here one may have to acknowledge greater weight for beliefs and attitudes and traditions. Still later it considers the nature of religious traditions from several angles, dilating on the issue largely because it has been so sadly neglected over the decades. This review will clear the way for sketching, in conclusion, the context wherein communalism grew during the colonial period.

Another introductory note: it is the conflict, the adversary relations, phrased in terms of 'Hindu' and 'Muslim', which will be discussed here. This is not to deny that most Muslims and Hindus, most of the time, have lived with each other cordially, though in my judgement, reflected in the following analysis, intimate relations and confident understanding across this boundary have not been common; and behind the cordiality of public encounters, there has often been antagonism in private.[1] To acknowledge the last element is neither to justify it nor to accuse anyone for it; but to deny its scale and depth would amount to foreclosing any serious attempt at understanding communalism.

THE LITERATURE

Questions of power and of economic interests are inevitably implicated in communalism, but these will enter our discussion principally through the disciplines of sociology and history with which I have some familiarity.

Numerous studies of local communities, the staple of sociological research in India over the past generation, provide more or less detail about the nature of relations between Hindus and Muslims in their localities. The localities tended to be rural in the earlier years, as in the work by S. C. Dube (1955: 85, 111, 115, 187, 226 in Telengana), T. S. Epstein (1962: 32f in Karnataka), T. N. Madan (1972, in Kashmir), Partap Aggarwal (1971, in Rajasthan), and Marc Gaborieau (1972, in Nepal); and later work has often been on urban areas, as by Harold Gould (1974, in Faizabad, U.P.), Mattison Mines (1972, in Tamil Nadu), Christine Dobbin (1972, in Bombay in late nineteenth century), S. P. Jain (1975, in U.P.), and Lina Fruzzetti-Ostor (1972, in West Bengal). Principally anthropological in inspiration, this literature is certainly useful; yet there has been a singularly puzzling inability on our part to draw creatively upon the sociological tradition which arose with the nineteenth century attempt to interpret the social crisis

[1]My failure in this essay to take note of the countless syncretic beliefs, practices, and sects arises in the judgement that, during and after the colonial period, these syncretisms have proved to be rather weak in the face of resurgent Islamic and Hindu traditions and identities. Why this should have been so is a question for another occasion.

in Europe, one whose dimensions approach those of our own.[2]

Specially, Indian sociologists have been wary of questions which would have had to be asked of the published, secondary literature. Communal relations, ranging over time and space, are one such question. At this wider level we have Ramakrishna Mukherjee (1973) on developments in Eastern Bengal, and D. N. Dhanagare (1977) on the Moplahs; and, for both, the dimension of communal conflict is incidental to other interests. Beyond that, Yogendra Singh (1973) has a chapter on 'the impact of Islam and modernization'—marginal to our theme, but also much too uncertain about its authorities as well as its own analytic stance.[3]

One must note, finally, Louis Dumont's long, complex, and insightful paper, 'Nationalism and Communalism', an inquiry away from his central interests. The essay is built around critiques of the earlier writings of A. R. Desai, W. C. Smith and Beni Prasad, and finds the last the most congenial. A widespread tendency to assume the pre-eminence of economic factors in all situations strikes Dumont as the principal obstacle frustrating many earlier discussions of the question. Both the communities, says Dumont, had during the medieval period edged towards 'a compromise which depended for its maintenance on the continuance of Muslim power' (1964: 55). They lived together for centuries, generally peacefully, yet there was little fusion of their values; together they did not come to 'constitute a society'. During the nineteenth-century flux which attended the ongoing change of scale, political mobilization which appealed to sacred symbols, as Tilak's did, was necessarily separative in its effects; and because the Congress was unable to accommodate this great cleavage in its political vision and style, it could not secure Muslim support generally. Though

[2]See Nisbet (1966). Our difficulty has been due partly to the burial of much of this nineteenth-century sociological tradition under the rather dreary sands of formalized, quantified, scale-building survey research in the United States. The plain lesson is that we cannot escape the task of constructing our own sociology; and I suspect that we will find its materials in nineteenth-century sociology, in twentieth-century anthropology, and in a comparative study of the long-run Indian and Western historical experience.

[3]Illustratively, on authorities, consider n. 17a, on p. 65, for its adequacy to the context. On the analytic stance, Chs. 1 and 3 leave me wondering how Yogendra Singh sees Islam: a modernizing element in India owing to its 'heterogenetic' status, or a traditional one owing to an allegedly hierarchical spirit? Or are these not the right questions?

long neglected as an aberration by both sociologists and historians, Dumont's analysis is a necessary beginning for further work on the issue.[4]

Questions of communalism have a remarkably different cast in the historians' literature. At least some of a group of scholars writing in the 1960s appear to see communal antagonisms as a consequence substantially of tendentious historiography which has sought to put allegedly 'Hindu' or 'Muslim' constructions upon medieval and later events (I. Habib 1961; Thapar et al. 1969).[5] The erring scholars are not named, but may be guessed; and to an outsider it appears that they should be seen as *victims*—perhaps willing, perhaps unwitting—of a society which is rent by antagonistic communal attitudes, as scholars who understand the social process too little to shed the prejudices they share with their neighbours: and not as *culprits* responsible for the fact of communalism: its cultural roots are very much older than the corpus of modern historiography, though the latter undoubtedly is an element in the milieu.

This critique of communal historiography was Marxian in inspiration, and it has certainly been influential in the social sciences in India over the past generation; yet its analytic logic has virtually no place for such categories as 'Hindu' and 'Muslim', or for the associated cultural traditions and needs, conscious and unconscious, that these meet.

In relation to this historiography, Mushirul Hasan's *Nationalism and Communal Politics in India* (1979) is poised uneasily. Marxian in conviction, in epigraph, and in occasional interpretation, Hasan is not shy of the categories Hindu and Muslim and offers perhaps the most satisfactory analysis yet of communal politics, focussing on developments before, during, and after the Khilafat and Non-Cooperation, and outlining the road to 1947. The Muslims were a category, divided internally by region, sect, and class; and it was the acceptance of the principle of communal representation, by the government in 1909 and by the Congress in 1916, and the subsequent enlargement of franchise in 1919 and 1935, that Professor Hasan sees as spurring on the communal and separatist politics. He is exceptional in his acute awareness of the power of

[4]Ratna Naidu's monograph (1980) appeared after the initial writing of this essay; I have reviewed it at length elsewhere (1981).

[5]Their project included the writing of the well known NCERT textbooks. reflecting the new historiography.

religious symbols and ideas, yet implicitly equates communalism with communal *politics*. The focus set thus, the explanation covers the period examined; but the sense of communal identity and the associated antagonisms, here manifest, there latent, have survived the end of separate electorates, and undoubtedly antedated their introduction.

The spur to communalism is located by Professor Bipan Chandra a generation or two earlier in the nineteenth-century competion for jobs, in the colonial universe of small opportunities in a potentially expansionary social scale, so that if claims to one's 'community's backwardness' and the like could confer additional leverage, these were eagerly brought into play (1984: 39–43 and *passim*). The attempt here is to locate the *'causes or factors in Indian society* responsible for [the growth of communalism] and for the stage-by-stage enlargement of its social base' (ibid. : 29; emphasis his); but while the various religious traditions and social experiences are noticed, the possible contribution of their mutual abrasiveness to communalism is virtually defined out of the analytic field.

It seems to me, however, that this competition for government jobs and the separation of electorates are causes too minor to account for the effects to be explained. A certain matching of magnitudes between causes and effects seems to be warranted. If the historian's fine sense of causation takes him to the spark that lights the tinder, the sociologist's gross sense draws him to the tinder instead; both are necessary for the fire to start.

I happen to be a sociologist; but before proceeding further, we should note that the social sciences in India in recent decades have been rather reluctant to take serious account of religious beliefs and institutions in any context, with the limited exception of some followers of Dumont. This reluctance, especially in India, demands anlaysis in its own right; and its implications for understanding communalism are sufficiently serious for it to be examined itself now. In the earlier pages we have reviewed some *academic* inhibitions to such interest; but wider influences have also been active, and these are considered in the Appendix (pp. 76 ff)..

INTERESTS AND TRADITIONS

I started out by suggesting that communal relations between

Hindus and Muslims have to be seen at several levels, ranging from a village to a ruling class. Such a phenomenon cannot be unitary or homogeneous, yet any of its specific expressions may be analysable over common conceptual ground, provided its categories have strategic fit. Here, as elsewhere, it is useful to consider the framework of *interests* separately from, as well as in relation to, the realm of *ideas*, which appear in this case as religious *traditions*.[6]

Both these realms, of interests and of ideas and traditions, are of course part of every social situation; and each has its own distinctive logic—of meaning, of coerciveness, and of the resources available for renewal; yet their separation is an analytic artifact. On the ground, all these usually constitute unseparated experience. In that experience, the religious traditions are transmitted and renewed in processes, social and cultural, which are both conscious and unconscious; and the latter is especially important for such societies (and persons) as do not habitually bring their own unconscious to the inquiring gaze of consciousness.

Framework of interests

Let us begin with the central Marxian recognition of the sociological reality—call it coerciveness—of the context in which human beings labour and of the mechanisms whereby the product of their labour is appropriated. For reasons that will become clear, however, we have to keep in mind not merely the work situation, agrarian or industrial, but the broader question of access to a mode of making a living, and of the defence of one's hold on that living; and for these one uses certain relationships which may thereby separate one's social universe into allies and adversaries and neutrals. This separation may be done in terms other than those of material interests alone, as we shall see.

Interests may come to be defined in several ways. During the early twentieth century, the cultivators in certain parts of Malabar and in eastern Bengal were Muslim, their landlords Hindu; and the conflict of *class* interests between them tended, or could be made, to look like communal conflict. (On Malabar: Dhanagare 1977, Panikkar 1979; on Bengal: R. Mukherjee 1973, Sarkar 1973:

[6]Cohen (1974) similarly places the interactions between relations of power and the symbolic order at the centre of the social process. I thank Josef Gugler for giving me a copy of this book.

443 *et seq.*) In certain parts of late nineteenth-century Punjab, differences of economic interests tended to coincide with differences of caste and also sometimes of religion (van den Dungen 1972, R. Smith 1971). More generally for the nineteenth century, P.C. Joshi (1980: 172–5) speaks of Muslim landowners steadily losing out to Hindu merchants and moneylenders; and this interface was not unknown during the medieval period. Situations of this kind express variously the common historical tendency in India for occupation to correspond with caste or ethnicity, with the proviso that in any particular case the link could have begun from the end either of occupation or of ethnicity. That is to say, *either* persons entering a particular occupation may constitute themselves into a caste—as in the historic cases of Rajputs and Kayasthas—*or* persons of a particular caste may move into the same occupation, as in a Punjabi town during the 1960s—the erstwhile leather-workers moving into lathework (Saberwal 1976: Ch. 5).

Change of religion has usually been not an individual but a collective matter, tending to associate caste with religion in any locality. Consequently, the internal social cement for occupational groups in adversary economic relations often consists indistinguishably of caste and religious ties. Where the two identities, say of Hindus and Muslims, are separated by the coincident boundaries of occupation, caste, and religion, the religious symbols may come to the fore by virtue merely of their mobilizational potential; but, as in the Moplah conflicts, men of religion may also be catalytic, or more active, in channelling what may otherwise seem to be 'purely' class interests.

Communal identities may however be implicated not only in *class* conflict but also in what, for want of an established term, may be called the *competitive* conflict of interests within a 'class'. It arises over access to a given array of opportunities; and we have noted that Bipan Chandra sees the competition for government jobs in late 1800s as pivotal to the later emergence of communalism in colonial politics. The boundary seen to be activated here is the religious one (and similar anxiety is reported for the late 1500s and early 1600s among certain elements of the Mughal nobility).[7] However, to attribute this to 'false consciousness'

[7]This is the 'Naqshbandi reaction': A. Ahmad (1964: Ch. 7); Friedmann (1971).

(Chandra 1984: 18–22 and *passim*) seems to me to be an evalua-tion, not an explanation. A search for explanation merely turns the attribution into a further question: namely, what were the historical antecedents that made the 'false consciousness' emerge along this particular boundary much more than along others asso-ciated with such criteria as caste, region, rural/urban differences and so forth?

RELIGIOUS TRADITIONS

Religious identities, I have suggested, tend to get implicated in conflicts of interest, whether of the class or the competitive sorts; but why should religion be implicated in identities at all, and why should these identities engage each other so often in antagonistic terms? With this question our inquiry has to go on a long but unavoidable detour. The length of this detour is deliberate. It demarcates a limited, strategic domain to which we must attend, however strong our aversion to doing so may hitherto have been.

I see religion in the following pages as part of culture, viewed anthropologically. While a religious tradition can be integrative, of a social group as well as of the individual psyche, its symbolic order sometimes persuades its believers in various ways to set themselves apart from the followers of other traditions, laying the basis for communal identities. The transmission of religious traditions is associated with religious experience which is commonly not verbal-ized or even conscious. And where the religious identities have come to adversary arrays, their antagonisms are stored in the unconscious, in addition to their presence in individual consciousness and enact-ment in more or less public settings. The run of my analysis will thus force me to point towards the importance of the unconscious, however distant the latter be from my limited competence.

Culture and Religion

Culture here refers to the totality of more or less changing concep-tions concerning nature and society, self and others, past, present and future, which any functioning human group possesses, renews, and lives by. All cultural conceptions are ultimately man-made but most are inherited from one's own or others' ancestors, substan-tially organized into complexes of ideas and social relations; except in acutely disrupted societies, these complexes of ideas and relationships are received by the next generation carrying the marks of 'transcendental law-like necessity' (Bauman 1973: 76f);[8] much of the scepticism of our time is itself a cultural complex of ideas and relationships.

The human perception of whatever is observed is almost invariably mediated by culturally given conceptions.[9] What is culturally organized may be deliberately so by consciously acting human beings, resorting to culturally derived preferences and routines; but central to the modern understanding of society is the recognition that a great deal of this organization at any time may in fact be *un*conscious. Cultural conceptions are subject to continuous patterning and selecting, part of an often unconscious process of cultural integration.

The principles underlying the integration of culture are too varied to be considered here; I need only make a few simple points. Modern societies organize road traffic, *inter alia*, by specifying the side that the traffic should keep, but these rules are neutral to the travellers' states of ritual purity.[10] The Hindu tradition employed ideas of ritual purity and pollution to organize a great deal of the social traffic, but it tended to be neutral to a vast range of social observances, leaving the caste group largely free to manage its own affairs. Islam came to stress the importance of the *sunnah*, the beaten path of Islamic tradition, and expected its observance by every Muslim, by the entire *umma*, the entire community; but there is no Islamic law for organizing road traffic.[11] Through time and cumulative experience a culture comes to be centred upon

[8]Bauman (1973: 76f) presents something of the complex patterning in cultural phenomena and the complex formulations of the concept which prevail today.

[9]For the underlying theoretical tradition, see Rose (1962), especially the papers by Rose and Blumer. Admittedly, numerous situations are shaped by a logic so coercive as to permit one to simplify analysis by eliminating the interpretative mediation, e.g., the economic consequences of colonialism. In the case of *communalism*, however, interpretative mediation happens to be the heart of the matter.

[10]My choice of traffic rules to illustrate the cultural integration of modern societies is deliberate. It is characteristic of 'rationality' in these societies to devise rather simple rules to regulate various sorts of dense traffic—on rails, on radio waves, in the mails, in the air, and so forth. Cp. Hannerz (1980: 102).

[11]I owe my limited understanding of Islam to von Grunebaum (1955), Watt (1961), Rodinson (1971, 1974), Geertz (1968).

certain key ideas which have served recurrently in meeting a wide range of contingencies; these key ideas together may be said to constitute a culture's integrative core.

Until the secularist growth of the last two or three centuries, this integrative core in complex premodern societies invariably claimed transcendental origins, and the sanctions behind this core were widely believed to have transcendental legitimacy. Modern historiography is beginning to show that, at the time of the initial promulgation, the early ideas of some of the great religious traditions arose in sharp intuitive insight into the prophet's own social milieu, showing for example how to re-order the framework of social relations so as to accommodate the changing structures of interests more adequately.[12] In the prevailing struggle between competing sets of ideas, the evidence of a prophet's extraordinary experiences, possibly of the supernatural, would give his message an edge, sometimes decisively.

Later generations would amplify and systematize the prophet's message, but certain core symbols would run through and recognizably unify the inevitably vast diversities of the community of believers. Thus in Islam we have the Prophet as the Messenger of God; his sayings and actions as the roots of Islamic law; the sacred core in the Meccan shrines; the unity of the *umma*, the religious community, guided by the *ulema*, the religious scholars. When, say, the Haj brought together Muslims from Djakarta and Rabat, or from Calicut and Agra, they would recognize in each other a certain sharing of religious sensibilities, a bond that made them brothers in faith. This bond would be sensed by their neighbours at home, too, who only heard about the pilgrimage, and could not themselves make it.

This bond, we have to concede, is *not* commonly subjected to empirical judgements as to whether or not the mutual commonalities outweigh the mutual differences. It arises, rather, in faith, in the implicit acceptance of the symbolic order, which acts much of the time at more or less unconscious levels of experience: such elements as purity and pollution, the sanctity of the cow or the power of the Mother, the importance of conserving one's semen ... these elements are suffused through and are expressed in

[12]For the rise of Islam, both Rodinson (1971) and Watt (1961) write in these terms. For Buddha, likewise, D. D. Kosambi (1965: 104–13).

numerous seemingly unconnected areas of belief and experience.[13]
Each element in the symbolic order acquires its meaning within a
psychological universe, which is also an experienced universe; and
this meaning is created by the ceremonial, by recurrent experiences,
and by its confirmation by others during and outside these ceremonies and experiences. In a phrase, this experienced universe is also
a moral order. Its meanings are not available immediately outside
such a universe; but for the believer these are often critical in
intra-psychic integration, and their effectiveness is the greater for
their being unconscious.[14]

Religion and Communal Identity

In premodern societies the sense of community fostered in the
religious traditions would give direction to much of the prevailing
life-style. Imprinted on the child's mind is the sanctity of worship,
its place, words, gestures, sounds, smells, and personnel. Religious
acts and functionaries attend many of the critical episodes in life:
birth, illness, marriage, death. There are dietary injunctions: be a
vegetarian, eat only *halal* meat, beef may or may not be prohibited.
Key complexes of religious belief, with their organizing symbols,
are thus implanted during the *pre*-reflective years of childhood,
when one has little option but to accept one's elders' ideas without
question.[15] It would not have happened equally for everyone; but
it did happen in enough families to set the temper in their social
group. To one born into and surrounded by a faith, its *shared*
experiences, meanings, and gestures have the taken-for-granted
quality which underlies social ease; and therefore nearly all
marriages would have been made within the faith. It would have
also been an important basis for *separation* from the followers of
another faith—in worship, in religious education, in residence—

---

[13]At this point one has to read the psychoanalysts: Erikson (1970), Kakar
(1978), Masson (1980). Cp: 'The more meanings a symbol signifies, the more
ambiguous and flexible it becomes, the more intense the feelings it evokes, the
greater its potency, and the more functions it achieves.' This is from the
anthropologist Cohen (1974: 32). See also Berger and Luckmann (1966: 110ff).

[14]My comments draw upon personal experience of the Arya Samaj and
Quakers in India and in North America. Fieldwork among the Embu of
Central Kenya (1963–4) covered their beliefs concerning the supernatural too;
but my interest in the anthropological understanding of religion was aroused
only recently as I turned to the literature on Islam.

[15] This situation has concomitants: see p. 70, 74 below.

within the local community and, when the need arose, for a set of potential supra-local links for those who reached out.

A religious tradition, put otherwise, is or used to be like a compass, helping one chart a course through life. It used to be a sanctified manual, listing the do's and dont's for coping with the universe.[16] Members of a multireligious society, however, would work with different manuals, listing divergent codes for life. Where people lived by different manuals, one way to anticipate the other's behaviour, attitudes, and intentions would have been to reckon with the other's manual, the other's religion. Social unease could furthermore be obviated by signalling one's own manual, through various diacritical marks: clothing, hairstyle, facial marks, perhaps one's language and manners. Religiously rooted social identities would thus be established and be mutually acknowledged.

Awareness of the socio-religious identities, then, would help one constitute useful social maps in one's mind, demarcating the social territory into sacred, friendly, neutral, hostile, etc. These social maps are sometimes expressed in, and validated by, myths and legends. Marc Gaborieau (1972: 92f) reports the transformation of a seventh-century event in central Iraq into a religious myth in the hills of Nepal:

> ... in the central hills, the martyrs Hasan and Husain are venerated during the ten first days of the lunar month of *Muharram*; further west the fair of Ghazi Miyan is held in the beginning of the solar month *of Jesth* .... In actual history, Hasan and Husain were killed by Muslims, Ghazi Miyan by Hindus; but in the mind of the hill Muslims, the two legends blend curiously, and the story of the former is shaped on the same pattern as that of the latter: it runs briefly as follows.
>
> The heroes are Muslims: their marriage is going to take place and the rejoicing has begun to the sound of auspicious music. Suddenly there is news that the enemies, who are Hindus, are coming to attack; the auspicious music is changed into a martial music and the heroes, mounting their horses, rush to fight the enemies. They are finally killed and the story ends in lamentation and the funeral music.
>
> ... during *Muharram* and Ghazi Miyan fair [they] can express successively joy in evoking the marriage, aggression when they commemorate the battle in a sham fight, finally grief when

[16]This is a deliberately utilitarian stance on religion. For a modern, anthropological attempt to comprehend the ineffable in religion, see Geertz (1966, 1968).

they sing lamentations, for this legend tells of the greatest sorrow: death on the day of marriage. And one should emphasize that the main theme of those festivities, where Muslims express themselves without restraint, is an irreducible enmity between Hindus and Muslims.

A traditional account undergoes transformation in the course of meeting the conscious and unconscious needs of those who recite it and thus comes to reflect their social maps of their universe. A traditional recital defining a group as hostile thus renews its status as an adversary, and such definitions persist when the corresponding expectations are confirmed episodically in experience (e.g., ibid.: 93).

These social maps remain much in use even when the latter-day secular understandings of nature and society, of life and death, and of one's inner world make one sceptical of the received religious manual and its transcendental aura.

Religious Traditions and the Unconscious

Religious grounding used to be, and often continues to be, important for identities which constitute the social maps for regulating *public* social relations; and it so happens that similarly grounded devices also provide the means for coping with and for organizing the *inner* worlds.[17] I proceed now to sketch the connections in the latter direction.

While the exigencies of life are infinitely variable, some of the key themes in any society arise as its cultural resources and constraints are used for canalizing instinctual impulses—including those of sexuality—and for coping with the trauma left over from childhood. The enormous importance of these devices for the individual psyche is being attested by the slowly growing psychoanalytic work on Indian cultural materials (Kakar 1978, Masson 1980). These historically created devices—austerities, devotions, pilgrimages— are options available *within* a tradition; and just as many of the traumas and instinctual difficulties arise in the ongoing functions and malfunctions of society, so too their bearers take to these devices selectively, recurrently. The point to note here is that a great many of these devices for creating order within one's private self appear to be embedded intimately in the meanings and symbols

[17]There is also the tiny minority able to live largely by the modern, secular understanding of these matters.

associated *contrastively* with the several religious traditions. These core psychological and cultural devices also would sustain the social separation.

The use of communal identities by the unconscious at another level was called to my attention by Sudhir Kakar, the psychoanalyst, drawing upon his own fieldwork at Balaji's temple, off Bharatpur in Rajasthan. From various parts of North India—Bihar, Punjab, Rajasthan and elsewhere—persons with mental disturbance, usually considered to be possessed by a spirit, a *bhuta*, come to the temple for its curative rituals. During these rituals, the spirit, 'speaking' through the patient, is persuaded to reveal its own identity and attributes. In the culture surrounding the temple, 'Muslim *bhutas* are considered to be the strongest and the most malignant of evil spirits, indicating perhaps the psychological depths of the antipathy between Hindus and Muslims' (Kakar 1982: 63). In the categories of this social context, the Muslim belongs with the untouchable:[18]

> *bhangiwara* . . . specializes in dealing with the Muslim *bhuta* and [spirits from] the untouchable castes. When a patient comes out of the *bhangiwara* enclosure after having exorcised one of these *bhutas*, it is imperative that he take a ritual bath to rid himself of the pollution. Otherwise it is held that if the patient touches someone else after his *bhangiwara* sojourn, it is almost certain that his *bhuta* will be transferred to the other person (1982: 60).

Translating the healing, exorcising routines at the temple into modern psychotherapeutic terms, Kakar sees these as strengthening:

> attempts to transform the patient's belief into a conviction that his bad traits and impulses are not within but without; that they are not his own but belong to the *bhuta*. The fact that fifteen out of twenty-eight patients were possessed by a Muslim spirit indicates the extent of this projection in the sense that the Muslim seems to be *the* symbolic representation of the alien in the Hindu unconscious. Possession by a Muslim *bhuta* reflects the patient's desperate efforts to convince himself and others that his hungers for forbidden foods, tumultuous sexuality, and uncontrollable rage belong to the Muslim destroyer of taboos and are farthest away from his 'good' Hindu self (1982: 87).

[18]Apparently connected with the logic of purity and pollution, this equation is rather widespread: e.g., Khare (1976: p. 249 and *passim*). See discussion later.

Interpreting the unconscious is a highly specialized field, one for
which I have no credentials; yet nearly a century after Freud the
sociologist must willy-nilly come to terms with this domain. He
has to reckon with the interconnectedness of the social, the conscious, and the unconscious; and this applies to the phenomenon
of communal separativeness too. The analysis continues with the
social organization of religious traditions and communal identities.

Social Organization of Tradition

It is not merely beliefs and symbols and myths but also, as Redfield (1956) and Singer (1964) pointed out, a social organization
that makes a tradition: religious specialists, temples, traditional
schools, ceremonies and recitations, sacred centres, networks,
pilgrimages and the like. Important for us are the links between
localities which arise in this social organization. In a world of
small, often defensive communities, the religious specialist, itinerant or resident, with his literacy and wider connexions and
awareness of the sacred and sometimes secular literature, has
been the man interpreting new situations, appealing to prior
categories and symbols, and sometimes re-sacralizing hitherto
dormant ones. My illustrations of these inter-local connexions,
actual and potential, come from the colonial period.[19] Mushirul
Hasan has reviewed how the *ulema* helped to get the Khilafat
Movement going:

> They took the lead in voicing Muslim concern over Turkey
> and the Holy Places and, after 1918, they seized the initiative
> from the Muslim League leaders, thus unleashing forces of
> vast political consequence. Fired by religion and buoyed up
> by their romantic sympathy for the Turkish *Khalifa* they
> carried pan-Islamic ideology to town and countryside where
> in mosque and *maktab*, Muslim artisans, weavers, and peasants
> were susceptible to their religious exhortations. They used the
> Quran and the *Hadith* as powerful weapons to gain adherence
> of the faithful who accepted them as infallible. They also
> forged an alliance with Muslim professional men and utilized
> their experience in agitational politics to further the cause of
> Pan-Islamism (1979: 307).

Or consider the late nineteenth-century campaigns in Lahore and
Allahabad in support of reviving the Vedas, encouraging *shuddhi*,

[19]For medieval analogues of these relatively insulated inter-local connections, see Rizvi (1977: 24–30), Sarma (1966).

protecting the cow, and propagating Hindi (K. Jones 1976; Bayly 1975). Meanings and symbols—Quran and *Hadith*, Vedas and the cow—emotionally charged and exclusively bounded. Such potent, symbolic elements lie across the psychic, the social, and the cultural, and, for many, at the core of social identities and religious traditions. We have noted earlier that these traditions are maintained and renewed in complexes of specialists, institutions, pilgrimages, literature, and so forth. These socio-religious webs have vast inter-local spreads, but few inter-connexions *across* the religious boundaries. Altogether, these tend to be separative.

THE RISE OF COMMUNALISM

Let us take stock of my argument. I have outlined the experiential bases of religious belief and identity, the use of religious identities to organize one's social space, the play of religiously embedded mechanisms in the run of one's inner life, and finally the separativeness of the inter-local networks within what have been called the Great Traditions of the historic civilizations. In settings where the religious symbolic order pervades the daily round, there would seem to be a widespread tendency for religious traditions to try to insulate these symbolic orders from each other by way of both residential separation and careful social routines. This tendency would be expressed categorically at the core of religious experiences and activities and more or less ambiguously in the more secular pursuits.

I move now to the milieu of the 1700s and the 1800s and consider the rise of communalism during this period, trying merely to indicate the major processes which appear to have fostered this growth.

I begin with everyday social relations. To the general tendency to religious separativeness, noted earlier, medieval India appears to have added:

1. the inter-cultural social distance between non-Indian immigrants and the natives, until time and circumstance combined to induce a measure of intimacy, at least in the ruling circles; and

2. the stigma of untouchability carried by the lower castes, whose conversion to Islam would scarcely remove that stigma, especially in their localities of origin. On the contrary, it seems

that for Hindus both the general tendency to religious separativeness and the specific antagonisms, consequent to loss of power, came to be set in the idiom and the routines of this untouchability.

From the medieval encounter there seems to have been inherited a social separation, sometimes hardened into patterns of residence, commensality, dress, and other acts of daily living. Yet the village community or the small town had relatively stable populations, and the marks of separation would have been taken for granted in an easy, daily round of life, where the caste order accommodated other sorts of separation too. This situation prevailed until, as we shall see, the setting began to shift in the 1800s.

Secondly, it is important to remember that Hindus, in numbers which grew with time, had high places in the ranks of the later medieval nobility (M. Habib 1958: 229f; Athar Ali 1968). In this political structure there were numerous relationships between Muslims and Hindus wherein the differences of their religious affiliations were in some measure set apart from the secular political and administrative tasks at hand. The sense of religious affiliation, which has commonly been central to the sense of one's identity, is ordinarily acquired during childhood, in the course of *primary* socialization, as we saw earlier. Affiliation in political, administrative, economic and similar contexts, in contrast, is ordinarily learned much later, during adolescence or adulthood in the course of *secondary* socialization. During the 1700s, the Mughal politico-administrative structure got dismantled, and its constitutive relationships tended to lapse; and in so far as these had previously acted in counterpoint to the separative religious and social relationships, rooted in primary socialization, which continued relatively undisturbed, henceforth the separative relationships would come into play without this secondary set of moderating influences.

Thirdly, as we have noted in earlier chapters, during the 1800s, *the social framework was beginning to grow in scale*. This process was embodied in part in the expanding metropolitan centres. In the older localities—villages and small towns—the social separation of various caste-like groups was cross-cut by the necessity for co-operation in agriculture, commerce, and so forth, and a corresponding involvement in mutual ceremonials (Aggarwal 1971: Ch. 9; Mines 1972: 102f); but migrants into the metropolitan centres have commonly travelled along the social corridors of kinship,

caste, etc. (Rowe 1973; Timberg 1978: Sec. C). The metropolis of
the 1800s and early 1900s appears to have been organized so that
rather large areas were relatively homogeneous as to religious
community. The prior sense of social separation carried by the migrants with them tended to be confirmed as they settled into these
larger, relatively homogeneous areas.[20] This pattern of metropolitan
residences is important not only for the consciousness of religious
community fostered in them, but also for the long-run, fitful influence of metropolitan models and messages on the lesser communities over the next century and more.

To sum up, I am suggesting that the rise of communalism during
the colonial period should perhaps be seen in relation to the long-
standing separativeness of religious networks, the acute social distance expressing a high level of social antagonism between Muslims
and Hindus, the lapse of formerly functioning, integrative political
and administrative ties, and the growth of communally homogeneous neighbourhoods in the new metropolitan centres.

It is in this historic context that we notice the conflicts of interests—class or competitive—which have in numerous localities often
pitted, or been seen to have pitted, groups of different religious
affiliations one against the other.[21] When, during the 1800s, with
expanding scales of some social relations, the inter-local linkages
of a *secular* sort began to expand vastly, this process built upon
the pre-existing social matrices, realigning these for their resources
and their influence in the changing milieu (Saberwal 1979). This
process did not often violate the boundaries of exclusion which
had been associated with the religious identities, and had been built
into vast regions of the prevailing styles of life. In ever changing

[20]On Calcutta, Siddiqui (1973), Bose (1968); on Bombay, M. Kosambi (1980:
121–36). On Allahabad, a *much older* city, Bayly (1975: 39–46) suggests for the
late 1800s a considerable admixture of Hindus and Muslims.

[21]*Within* the social organization of a religious tradition or of a communal
identity, too, there are interests to defend: those of the specialists in the organization, or of outsiders able to influence or control them, or, more likely, of
both. In defence of these more limited interests too, the specialists may try,
covertly if necessary, to mobilize the believers. It would be wholly wrong,
however, to dismiss such organizations simply as groups of self-servers. It is
characteristic of any enduring complex tradition, and of the associated identities, that these can generate individuals and groups committed to defending
the integrity of the tradition, and of identity, regardless of personal cost: that
is very much the stuff of martyrdom—a prolific source for fresh symbols!

manifestations, it was this combination of interests with inherited, antagonistic, social separation which became the basis for the *social organization of communal identities*. This social organization includes such elements as educational institutions, social service organizations, political and quasi-political formations, journals, ceremonies, and so forth. Somewhat detached from religious belief, yet religiously rooted, these 'communal' identities gathered strength as the wider social and political arenas came into being.

With older restraints weakening, and newer linkages forming separately in an era of unprecedented economic shifts, what had once been relatively stable, largely local interfaces between Hindus and Muslims tended to become much wider and more active oppositions. Of this situation, the colonial regime was at times more than willing to take advantage (e.g., Sarkar 1973: 8–20).[22]

APPENDIX

Religion and the Social Sciences

Despite their varied persuasions, the social sciences in India, for a generation now, have tended to be dismissive of religious matters but, unfortunately, such an attitude has helped neither to improve our understanding, nor to reduce the power, of the phenomena so dismissed. This attitude has not been problematical—one takes it for granted.

In retrospect, this attitude seems to have been associated with a scientific, secular world-view noticeable in at least some areas in Indian society. For one who takes this latter world-view seriously, it can mean something of a break with the ancestral faith, which can be seen to be threatening by one's kin—and it may add up to a struggle in the family. Yet decay in ancestral religious observances has, in recent decades, come to be tolerated relatively well, and one settles for an easy agnosticism, taking on a rather passive identity as one or another sort of Muslim or Hindu or Christian, without an active search for rigorous belief, religious or secular. In reducing one's uncertainty levels, the prevailing routines seem to spur us into intensified social relations rather than critically won

[22]The wedge would look, of course, for whatever cleavages happened to be there in a region: thus the Brahmin/Non-Brahmin divide in Madras.

beliefs and impersonal strategies. Above all, the operative premise seems to be that 'religion' is not to be taken seriously. The word connotes communal riots, meaningless ritual, and a surrender to blind faith by those unable to cope with a crisis. Robust minds, we presume, need no religious beliefs. To take serious interest in these would be to admit one's own weakness—to others and to oneself.[23]

There are even greater difficulties in relation to religious traditions other than one's ancestral one. The medieval tradition of the relations between Hindus and Muslims was a mixed bag, and it has left its mark on the tenor of communal relations. Religious encounters during the 1800s, however, came to be charged with anxieties of another sort. Whereas Europe in the 1700s had sustained the inquisitiveness of the Renaissance about things alien, the 1800s opened with a lowering of the cultural shutters, as Europe's industrial sinews grew to guarantee her political dominance over Asia (e.g. Dumont 1976: last section). The evangelicals became more aggressive in Europe (Thompson 1963: Ch. II) and in India (Stokes 1959: 27ff). As the nineteenth century grew, the din of religious competitiveness became more raucous in India (Kopf 1969: Chs. 14–15; K. Jones 1976). The struggle for souls led by Christian missionaries put the other religious traditions very much on the defensive.

Christian missionary institutions were, however, often rated high for their educational calibre, and Hindu or Muslim parents sent their children to them; yet they sought to guard them against alien religious influence (Webster 1976: 150ff).[24] Any serious interest in a religious tradition other than the familial would be perceived to be threatening by one's group of origin; for should it lead to a change of faith, it would mean a virtually total breach in the convert's relations with the group of origin.[25] The coexistence

[23]This is not a necessary position. Clifford Geertz, an atheist, has worked on religious beliefs, and so have E. E. Evans-Pritchard and Victor Turner, both practising Roman Catholics. Observation of one's own private search for meaning—if it abides by the elementary rules of accurate observation—can enrich one's public accounts of the nature of religious experience.

[24]Much of the guarding would have been via the attitudes instilled during the child's earlier socialization.

[25]Illustratively, Conlon (1977: 79–84) documents the turmoil among Saraswat Brahmans in Mangalore following several such conversions in 1843 and 1862.

of numerous religious traditions in India has by and large meant
not mutual interest and curiosity but insulation and indifference.
These latter attitudes few of us have been able to outgrow; and
without the will to understand in a relaxed manner the inner logic
of the different religious traditions, how can one grasp the dynamic
of their mutual relations?

REFERENCES

Aggarwal, Partap, 1971, *Caste, Religion and Power.* New Delhi: Shri Ram Centre for Industrial Relations.

Ahmad, Aziz, 1964, *Studies in Islamic Culture in the Indian Environment.* Oxford: Clarendon Press.

Ali, M. Athar, 1968, *The Mughal Nobility under Aurangzeb.* Bombay: Asia Publishing House.

——, 1978, 'Towards an interpretation of the Mughal empire', *Journal of Royal Asiatic Society*, no. 1, pp. 38–49.

——, 1982, 'Theories of sovereignty in Islamic thought in India', Paper presented at Indian History Congress, Kurukshetra.

Anderson, Perry, 1974, *Lineages of the Absolutist State.* London: New Left Books.

Appadurai, Arjun, 1981, *Worship and Conflict under Colonial Rule.* Cambridge: Cambridge University Press.

Bauman, Zygmunt, 1973, *Culture as Praxis.* London: Routledge and Kegan Paul.

Bayly, C. A., 1975, *Local Roots of Indian Politics.* London: Oxford University Press.

Berger, Peter and Thomas Luckmann, 1966, *Social Construction of Reality.* Harmondsworth: Penguin.

Bidney, David, 1946, 'The concept of cultural crisis', *American Anthropologist*, 48: pp. 534–52. Reprinted in part as Ch. 12 in his *Theoretical Anthropology*. New York: Columbia University Press.

Bloch, Marc, 1961, *Feudal Society*, 2 vol. (tr. by L. A. Manyon). London: Routledge and Kegan Paul.

Bohannon, Paul, 1965, 'The differing realms of the law', *American Anthropologist*, v. 67, no. 6, pt. 2, pp. 33–42.

Bose, N. K., 1968, *Calcutta: A Social Survey.* Bombay: Lalvani Publishers.

Brennan, Lance, 1977, 'From one raj to another: Congress politics in Rohilkhand, 1930–1950'. *In* D. A. Low (ed.), *Congress and the Raj: facets of the Indian Struggle 1917–47.* London: Heinemann, pp. 473–503.

Buck, Mark, 1983, *Politics, Finance and the Church in the Reign of Edward II: Walter Stapeldon, Treasurer of England.* Cambridge: Cambridge University Press.

Carstairs, G. Morris, 1957, *The Twice-born: A Study of High-Caste Hindus.* Bombay: Allied Publishers (1971 reprint).

Chandra, Bipan, 1984, *Commnnalism in Modern India.* New Delhi: Vikas Publishing House.

Chattopadhyaya, B. D., 1976, 'Origins of the Rajputs: the political, economic, and social processes in early medieval Rajasthan', *Indian Historical Review*, 3: 59–82.

Cipolla, C. M., 1972 (ed.), *The Fontana Economic History of Europe: The*

Middle Ages, London: Collins Publishers.

Cohen, Abner, 1974, *Two Dimensional Man*. London: Routledge and Kegan Paul.

Conlon, Frank, 1977, *A Caste in a Changing World: The Chitrapur Saraswat Brahmans 1700–1935*. Berkeley: University of California Press.

Das Gupta, Jyotirindra, 1981, *Authority, Priority and Human Development*. Delhi: Oxford University Press.

Dhanagare, D. N., 1977, 'Agrarian conflict, religion, and politics: The Moplah rebellions in Malabar in the 19th and early 20th centuries', *Past and Present*, 74: pp. 112–41.

Dirks, N. B., 1976, 'Political authority and structural change in early South Indian history', *Indian Economic and Social History Review*, 13: pp. 125–57.

Dobbin, Christine, 1972, *Urban Leadership in Western India: Politics and Communities in Bombay City, 1840–85*. Oxford: Oxford University Press.

Dodwell, H. H., (ed.), 1929, *The Cambridge History of India, V.5, British India 1497–1858*. Cambridge: Cambridge University Press.

Dube, S. C., 1955, *Indian Village*. London: Routledge and Kegan Paul.

—— (ed.), 1977, *India since Independence: Social Reports on India 1947–72*. New Delhi: Vikas Publishing House.

Duby, Georges, 1980, *The Three Orders: Feudal Society Imagined* (tr. from French by A. Goldhammer). Chicago: University of Chicago Press.

——, 1981, *The Age of the Cathedrals: Art and Society 980–1420* (tr. from French by E. Levieux and B. Thompson). Chicago: University of Chicago Press.

Dumont, Louis, 1957, 'For a sociology of India', *Contributions to Indian Sociology*, 1: pp. 8–22.

——, 1964, 'Nationalism and communalism', *Contributions to Indian Sociology*, 7: pp. 30–70.

——, 1965, 'The functional equivalents of the individual in caste society', *Contributions to Indian Sociology*, 8: pp. 85–99.

——, 1970a, *Homo Hierarchicus* (English tr., Paladin Books, 1972).

——, 1970b, 'The individual as an impediment to sociological comparison and Indian history'. *In* L. Dumont, *Religion/Politics and History in India*. Paris: Mounton Publishers, pp. 133–50.

——, 1976, 'The British in India'. *In* C. Moraze (ed.), *The Nineteenth Century* (UNESCO history of mankind, vol. 5, pt. 4). London: Allen & Unwin, pp. 1084–1141.

Dumont, Louis and D. Pocock, 1957, 'Village studies', *Contributions to Indian Sociology*, 1: pp. 23–41.

Elias, Norbert, 1978, '*The Civilising Process: History of Manners* (tr. from *Uber den Prozess der Zivilisation*, 1939, by Edmund Jephcott). Oxford: Basil Blackwell.

Epstein, T. S., 1962, *Economic Development and Social Change in South India*. Manchester: Manchester University Press.

Erickson, Carolly, 1976, *The Medieval Vision: Essays in History and Perception*. New York: Oxford University Press.

Erikson, Erik, 1970, *Gandhi's Truth*. London: Faber & Faber.

Fox, R. G., 1971, *Kin, Clan, Raja, and Rule: State-hinterland Relations in Pre-*

industrial India. Berkeley: Univers it v of California Press.

Frankel, Francine, R., 1978, *India's Political Economy 1947-77: the Gradual Revolution.* Delhi: Oxford University Press.

Friedmann, Yohann, 1971, *Shaykh Ahmad Sirhindi.* Montreal: McGill-Queen's.

Fruzzetti-Ostor, Lina, 1972, 'The idea of community among West Benga Muslims'. *In* P. Bertocci (ed.), *Prelude to Crisis.* Michigan State University: Centre for South and East Asian Studies, Occ. paper No. 80.

Furer-Haimendorf, C. v., 1967, *Morals and Merit: A Study of Values and Social Controls in South Asian Societies.* London: Weidenfeld and Nicolson.

Gaborieau, Marc, 1972, 'Muslims in the Hindu kingdom of Nepal', *Contributions to Indian Sociology*, n.s. 6: pp. 84–105.

Geertz, Clifford, 1966, 'Religion as a cultural system'. *In* M. Banton (ed.), *Anthropological Approaches to the Study of Religion.* London: Tavistock Publishers.

——, 1968, *Islam Observed: Religious Development in Morocco and Indonesia.* New Haven: Yale University Press.

——, 1973, 'Thick description'. *In* his *Interpretation of Cultures.* New York: Basic Books, pp. 3–30.

Giddens, Anthony, 1979, *Central Problems in Social Theory: Action, Structure and Contradiction in Social Analysis.* London: Macmillan Press.

Gould, Harold, 1974, 'The emergence of modern Indian politics: political development in Faizabad—pt. 1, 1884–1935', *Journal of Commonwealth and Comparative Politics*, 12: pp. 20–41.

Gurvitch, Georges, 1971, *Social Frameworks of Knowledge* (tr. Margaret A. Thompson and Kenneth A. Thompson), Oxford: Blackwell (original in French, 1966).

Habib, Irfan, 1961, [Symposium: the contribution of Indian historians to the process of national integration:] Medieval period, *Indian History Congress, Proceedings*, 24: pp. 350–57.

Habib, Mohammad, 1958, 'Life and thought of Ziauddin Barani', *Medieval India Quarterly*, 3: pp. 197–252.

——, 1974 (v. 1) and 1981 (v. 2), *Politics and Society During the Early Medieval Period: Collected Works* (ed. K. A. Nizami). New Delhi: People's Publishing House, 2 v.

Hannerz, Ulf, 1980, *Exploring the City: Inquiries Towards an Urban Anthropology.* New York: Columbia University Press.

Hardgrave, Robert L. Jr., 1969, *The Nadars of Tamilnadu: The Political Culture of a Community in Change.* Berkeley: University of California Press.

Hardy, Peter, 1976, [Decline of the Mughal empire:] Commentary and Critique, *Journal of Asian Studies*, 35: pp. 257–63.

——, 1978, 'The growth of authority over a conquered political elite', *In* J. F. Richards, 1978b, pp. 192–214.

Hasan, Ibn, 1936, *The Central Structure of the Mughal Empire.* New Delhi: Munshiram Manoharlal Publishers (1970 reprint).

Hasan, Mushirul, 1979, *Nationalism and Communal Politics in India.* New Delhi: Manohar Publishers.

Hasan, S. Nurul, 1943, 'The *mahzar* of Akbar's reign', *Journal of U.P. Historical Society*, 16: pp. 125–37.

Holmes, George, 1975, *Europe: Hierarchy and Revolt, 1320–1450*. Fontana: Collins Publishers.

Homans, George C., 1950, *The Human Group*. New York: Harcourt, Brace and World Inc.

Hopkins, Keith, 1968, 'Structural differentiation in Rome (200–31 BC), the genesis of an historical bureaucratic society'. *In* I. M. Lewis (ed.), *History and Social Anthropology*. London: Tavistock Publishers, pp. 63–79.

Ikram, S. M., 1964, *Muslim Civilization in India*. New York: Columbia University Press.

Inden, Ronald B., 1976, *Marriage and Rank in Bengali Culture : A History of Caste and Clan in Middle Period Bengal*. New Delhi: Vikas Publishing House.

Jain, S. P., 1975, *The Social Structure of Hindu-Muslim Community*. Delhi: National Publishers.

Johnson, Paul, 1976, *A History of Christianity*. London: Weidenfeld and Nicolson.

Jones, E. L., 1981, *The European Miracle: Environments, Economies, and Geopolitics in the History of Europe and Asia*. Cambridge: Cambridge University Press.

Jones, Kenneth W., 1976, *Arya Dharm*. New Delhi: Manohar Publishers.

Joshi, P. C., 1980, 'The economic background of communalism in India'. *In* B. R. Nanda (ed.), *Essays in Modern Indian History*. Delhi: Oxford University Press, pp. 167–81.

Kakar, Sudhir, 1978, *The Inner World*. Delhi: Oxford University Press.

———, 1982, *Shamans, Mystics and Doctors : A Psychological Enquiry into India and its Healing Traditions*. Delhi: Oxford University Press.

Kaul, J. N., 1974, *Higher Education in India, 1951–71: Two Decades of Planned Drift*. Simla: Indian Institute of Advanced Study.

Kaviraj, Sudipta, 1984, 'On the crisis of political institutions in India', *Contributions to Indian Sociology*, 18: pp. 223–43.

Khan, I. A., 1972, 'The Turko-Mongol theory of kingship', *Medieval India: A Miscellany*, II. Bombay: Asia Publishing House, pp. 8–18.

Khare, R. S., 1976, *Hindu Hearth and Home*. Delhi: Vikas Publishing House.

Kopf, David, 1969, *British Orientalism and the Bengal Renaissance*. Berkeley: University of California Press.

Kosambi, D. D., 1965, *Culture and Civilization of Ancient India in Historical Outline*. London: Routledge and Kegan Paul.

Kosambi, Meera, 1980, *Bombay and Poona: A Socio-ecological Study of Two Indian Cities 1650–1900*. University of Stockholm doctoral dissertation.

Kothari, Rajni, 1983, 'The crisis of the moderate state and the decline of democracy'. *In* Peter Lyon and James Manor (eds.) *Transfer and Transformation: Political Institutions in the New Commonwealth. Essays in Honour of W. H. Morris-Jones*. Leicester: Leicester University Press, pp. 29–47.

Le Goff, Jacques, 1972, 'The town as an agent of civilisation 1200–1500', *In* Cipolla, pp. 71–106.

———, 1980, *Time, Work, and Culture in the Middle Ages*. Chicago: University of Chicago Press.

Madan, T. N., 1972, 'Religious ideology in a plural society: the Muslims and

Hindus of Kashmir, *Contributions to Indian Sociology*, n.s. 6: pp. 106–41.

Malamoud, Charles, 1981, 'On the rhetoric and semantics of purusartha', *Contributions to Indian Sociology*, 15: pp. 33–54.

Mallett, Michael, 1971, *The Borgias: The Rise and Fall of a Renaissance Dynasty*. London: Paladin Books.

Mandelbaum, David G., 1970, *Society in India*. Bombay: Popular Prakashan (1972 reprint).

Mangat Rai, E. N., 1973, *Commitment My Style: Career in the Indian Civil Service*, Delhi, Vikas Publishing House.

Manor, James, 1983, 'Anomie in Indian politics: origins and potential wider impact', *Economic and Political Weekly*, 18, pp. 725–34.

Masson, J. Moussaieff, 1980, *The Oceanic Feeling*. Dordrecht (Holland): C. Reidel.

Mayer, Adrian, 1960, *Caste and Kinship in Central India*. Berkeley: University of California Press.

Mehrotra, S. R., 1971, *The Emergence of the Indian National Congress*. Delhi: Vikas Publishing House.

Mines, Mattison, 1972, *Muslim Merchants: The Economic Behaviour of an Indian Muslim Community*, New Delhi: Sri Ram Centre for Industrial Relations.

Minturn, Leigh and John T. Hitchcock, 1966, *The Rajputs of Khalapur, India*. New York: John Wiley.

Mukherjee, Ramkrishna, 1970, 'Study of social change and social development in the "developing societies" ', *Economic and Political Weekly*, 5, pp. 1159–70.

———, 1973, 'Social Background of Bangladesh'. *In* K. Gough and H. P. Sharma (eds.), *Imperialism and Revolution in South Asia*. New York: Monthly Review Press.

———, 1977, *Trends in Indian Sociology*, Monograph, vol. 25, no. 3, in *Current Sociology*.

Mukhia, Harbans, 1976, *Historians and Historiography During the Reign of Akbar*. New Delhi: Vikas Publishing House.

Murray, Alexander, 1978, *Reason and Society in the Middle Ages*. Oxford: Clarendon Press.

Naidu, Ratna, 1980, *The Communal Edge to Plural Societies: India and Malaysia*. New Delhi: Vikas Publishing House.

Nisbet, Robert A., 1966, *The Sociological Tradition* (1970 reprint). London: Heinemann.

Oommen, T. K., 1972, *Charisma, Stability and Change: An Analysis of Bhoodan-Gramdan Movement in India*. New Delhi: Thomson Press.

Panikkar, K. N., 1979, 'Peasant revolts in Malabar in the 19th and 20th centuries. *In* A. R. Desai (ed.), *Peasant Struggles in India*. Bombay: Oxford University Press, pp. 601–30.

Parry, J. P., 1979, *Caste and Kinship in Kangra*. New Delhi: Vikas Publishing House.

Pearson, M. N., 1976, 'Shivaji and the decline of the Mughal empire', *Journal of Asian Studies*, 35: pp. 221–35.

Perlin, Frank, 1981, 'The precolonial Indian state in history and epistemology'. *In* HJM Claessen and P. Skalnik (eds.), *The Study of the State*. The Hague:

Mouton, pp. 275–302.

Piltz, Anders, 1981, *The World of Medieval Learning* (tr. David Jones). Oxford: Blackwell.

Punalekar, S. P., 1981, *Aspects of Class and Caste in Social Tensions*: a *Study of Marathawad Riots*. Surat: Centre for Social Studies (mimeo).

Redfield, Robert, 1956, 'The social organization of tradition'. *In* his *Peasant Society and Culture*. Chicago: University of Chicago Press; also in J. M. Potter *et. al.* (eds.), *Peasant Society. A Reader*. Boston: Little Brown, 1967.

Reynolds, Susan, 1984, *Kingdoms and Communities in Western Europe, 900–1300*. Oxford: Clarendon Press.

Richards, Jeffrey, 1979, *Popes and Papacy in the Early Middle Ages, 476–752*. London: Routledge and Kegan Paul.

Richards, J. F., 1976, 'The imperial crisis in the Deccan', *Journal of Asian Studies*, 35: pp. 237–56.

——, 1978a, 'The formulation of imperial authority under Akbar and Jahangir'. *In* J.F. Richards, 1978b, pp. 252–85.

——, 1978b (ed.), *Kingship and Authority in South Asia*. Madison: Dept. of South Asian Studies, University of Wisconsin.

Rizvi, S. A. A., 1975, *Religious and Intellectual History of the Muslims in Akbar's Reign, 1556–1605*. New Delhi: Munshiram Manoharlal Publishers.

——, 1977, 'Islamic proselytisation' (7th to 16th centuries). *In* G. A. Oddie (ed.), *Religion in South Asia*. New Delhi: Manohar Publishers.

Rodinson, Maxime, 1971, *Mohammed*. London: Penguin Books.

——, 1974, *Islam and Capitalism*. London: Penguin Books.

Roethlisberger, F. J., 1977, *The Elusive Phenomena*: *An Autobiographical Account of My Work . . . .* Cambridge, Mass.: Harvard University Press.

Rose, A. M. (ed.), 1962, *Human Behaviour and Social Processes*: *An Interactionist Approach*, London: Routledge and Kegan Paul.

Roth, Guenther, 1979, 'Duration and Rationalization: Fernand Braudel and Max Weber'. *In* G. Roth and W. Schluchter, *Max Weber's Vision of History: Ethics and Method*. Berkeley: University of California Press, pp. 166–93.

Rowe, William L., 1973, 'Caste, kinship, and association in urban India'. *In* A. Southall (ed.), *Urban Anthropology*. New York: Oxford University Press, pp. 211–49.

Rudolph, Lloyd I., and Susanne Hoeber Rudolph, 1967, *The Modernity of Tradition*: *Political Development in India*. Chicago: University of Chicago Press.

Saberwal, Satish, 1976, *Mobile Men*: *Limits to Social Change in Urban Punjab*. New Delhi: Vikas Publishing House.

——, 1979, 'Inequality in colonial India', *Contributions to Indian Sociology*, 13: pp. 241–64.

——, 1981, 'Communalism: Indian/Malaysian, *Economic and Political Weekly*, 16: pp. 985–87.

——, 1982, 'On multiple codes', *Contributions to Indian Sociology*, 16: pp. 289–94.

——, 1985, 'Analysing the Indian social crisis: a personal chronicle', *Journal of Social and Economic Studies*, n.s., 2: pp. 223–41.

Sarkar, Sumit, 1973, *The Swadeshi Movement in Bengal 1903–1908*. New Delhi: People's Publishing House.

Sarma, S. N., 1966, *The Neo-Vaisnavite Movement and the Satra Institution of Assam*. Gauhati: Gauhati University.

Scammell, G. V., 1981, *The World Encompassed: The First European Maritime Empires, c. 800–1650*. London: Methuen.

Scruton, Roger, 1982, *Kant*. Oxford: Oxford University Press.

Shah, A. M., 1982, 'Division and Hierarchy: an overview of caste in Gujarat', *Contributions to Indian Sociology*, n.s., 16: pp. 1–33.

Sharma, G. D., 1977, *Rajput Polity: A Study of Politics and Administration of the State of Marwar 1638–1749*. New Delhi: Manohar Publishers.

Siddiqui, M. K. A., 1973, 'Caste among Muslims of Calcutta', *In* Imtiaz Ahmad (ed.), *Caste and Social Stratification Among the Muslims*. New Delhi: Manohar Publishers.

Simmel, Georg, 1908, 'How is society possible?' (tr. from German, K. H. Wolff, 1959). *In his On Individuality and Social Forms* (ed. by Donald N. Levine, 1971). Chicago: University of Chicago Press.

Singer, Milton, 1964, 'The social organization of Indian civilization', *Diogene*, no. 45, pp. 84–119; also in his *When a Great Tradition Modernizes*, 1972. Delhi: Vikas Publishing House.

———, 'Industrial leadership, the Hindu ethic, and the spirit of socialism'. *In his When a Great Tradition Modernizes*. Delhi: Vikas Publishing House, pp. 272–380.

Singh, Yogendra, 1973, *Modernization of Indian Tradition: A Systemic Study of Social Change*. Delhi: Thomson Press.

Smith, R. Saumarez, 1971, *Caste, Religion and Locality in the Punjab Census*. M. Litt. thesis, University of Delhi.

Southern, R. W., 1962, *Western Views of Islam in the Middle Ages*. Cambridge, Mass.: Harvard University Press.

Srinivas, M. N., 1952, *Religion and Society Among the Coorgs of South India*. Bombay: Asia Publishing House (1965 reprint).

SSRC (Social Science Research Council summer seminar on acculturation 1953), 1954, 'Acculturation: an exploratory formulation', *American Anthropologist*, 56, pp. 973–1002.

Steed, Gitel, 1955, 'Notes on an approach to a study of personality formation in a Hindu village in Gujarat'. *In* M. Marriott (ed.), *Village India*. Chicago: University of Chicago Press.

Stein, Burton, 1977, 'Temples in Tamil country, 1300–1750 AD', *Indian Economic and Social History Review*, 14: pp. 11–45.

———, 1980, *Peasant, State and Society in Medieval South India*. Delhi, Oxford University Press.

Stern, Henri, 1977, 'Power in traditional India: territory, caste and kinship in Rajasthan'. *In* R. G. Fox (ed.), *Realm and Region in Traditional India*, New Delhi: Vikas Publishing House, pp. 52–78.

Stokes, Eric, 1959, *English Utilitarians and India*. Oxford: Clarendon Press.

Tandon, Prakash, 1980, *Return to Punjab 1961–75*. New Delhi: Vikas Publishing House.

Taylor, Charles, 1975, *Hegel*, Cambridge: Cambridge University Press.

Tellenbach, Gerd, 1940, *Church, State and Christian Society at the Time of the Investiture Contest* (1970). New Jersey: Humanities Press.

Thapar, R., Mukhia, H., and Chandra, Bipan, 1969, *Communalism and the Writing of Indian History*. New Delhi: People's Publishing House.

Thomas, Keith, 1971, *Religion and the Decline of Magic: Studies in Popular Beliefs in 16th and 17th Century England*. Harmondsworth: Penguin Books (1973 ed.).

Thompson, E. P., 1963, *The Making of the English Working Class* (1968, Pelican ed.).

Thrupp, Sylvia, 1972, 'Medieval industry 1000-1500'. *In* Cipolla, pp. 221-73.

Timberg, Thomas A., 1978, *The Marwaris: From Traders to Industrialists*. New Delhi: Vikas Publishing House.

Trevor-Roper, H. R., 1967, *The European Witch-craze of the Sixteenth and Seventeenth Centuries and other Essays*. New York: Harper and Row Publishers.

Tripathi, R. P., 1964, *Some Aspects of Muslim Administration*. Allahabad: Central Book Depot.

Turner, Victor, 1974, 'Religious paradigms and political action: Thomas Becket at the Council of Northampton'. *In* his *Dramas, Fields, and Metaphors*. Ithaca: Cornell University Press, pp. 60-97.

Ullmann, Walter, 1955, *The Growth of Papal Government in the Middle Ages*. London: Methuen.

Van den Dungen, P. H. M., 1968, 'Changes in status and occupation in nineteenth century Punjab'. *In* D. A. Low (ed.), *Soundings in Modern South Asian History*. London: Weidenfeld and Nicolson, pp. 59-94.

———, 1972, *The Punjab Tradition*. London: Allen and Unwin.

von Grunebaum, G. E., (ed.), 1955, *Unity and Variety in Muslim Civilization*, Chicago: University of Chicago Press.

Wallace, Anthony F. C., 1957, 'Mazeway disintegration: the individual's perception of socio-cultural disorganization', *Human Organization*, 16: pp. 23-27.

———, 1961, *Culture and Personality*. New York: Random House.

Watt, Montgomery, 1961, *Islam and the Integration of Society*. London: Routledge and Kegan Paul.

Weber, Max, 1950, *General Economic History* (tr. F. H. Knight). New York: Collier Macmillan (1961).

———, 1968, *Economy and Society* (tr. G. Roth and C. Wittich). Berkeley: University of California Press (1978).

Webster, John C. B., 1976, *Christian Community and Change in 19th Century North India*. Delhi: Macmillan.

White, Jr., Lynn, 1972, 'The expansion of technology 500-1500'. *In* Cipolla, pp. 143-74.

Wilson, Godfrey and Monica, 1945, *The Analysis of Social Change: Based on Observations in Central Africa*. Cambridge: Cambridge University Press.

Ziegler, Norman P., 1973, *Action, Power and Service in Rajasthani Culture: A Social History of the Rajputs of Middle Period Rajasthan*. Chicago: University of Chicago, Ph.D. thesis.

———, 1978, 'Some notes on Rajput loyalties during the Mughal period. *In* J. F. Richards, 1978b, pp. 215-51.

INDEX

Abul Fazl 42f
Aggarwal, P. 59, 74
Ahmad, A. 45, 58, 64n
Akbar 7, 39, 42–5, 54, 55, 58
Alam, Muzaffar 41, 46
Ali, M. Athar 41, 43, 45, 54, 74
Anderson, P. 6, 10, 23, 47
anomie ix, 30ff, 34
anthropology x, 3, 59ff
Appadurai, A. 6, 21n, 28, 47, 51n, 52f
Aquinas, Thomas 15
Arabs 12, 14, 16, 55
Atal, Yogesh 25n
Auden, W. H. 11
Aurangzeb 22, 43, 44f
authority, *see* power

Badauni 45
Balban 41
Barani 3
Bauman, Z. 66n
Bayly, C. A. 73, 75n
Becket, Thomas 13
Bentham, Jeremy 24
Berger, P. 20, 68n
Bhattacharya, Sabyasachi 24n
Bindranwale, Jarnail Singh 30
bhoodan 25
Bidney, D. 3
Bloch, M. 13, 47, 56
Bohannan, P. 32n
Bose, N. K. 75n
brahmadeyas 48ff
Braudel, Fernand 4n
Brennan, L. 29f
Buck, M. 15n
bureaucracy 3, 10, 12, 23, 24, 27, 30,
    32, 34, 39, 45f, 48, 53, 55, 56

canon law 14
capitalism 3, 16, 24, 25, 33
Carolingians 13, 55
Carstairs, G. M. 36n

caste system 8, 19ff, 34, 64, 73ff
categorical imperative 33
cathedrals 16
Chandra, Bipan 62, 64
Chattopadhyaya, B. D. 37
Cholas 18, 28, 47–51
Cipolla, C. M. 13
clientship 37–40, 49, 52f, 54
Clive 23
clocks 16
codes 3f, 15, 17, 20, 22f, 24, 25, 32,
    46, 52, 56, 57; multiplicity of 20ff,
    27, 30f, 33, 39n, 40; *see also*
    Roman law; laws
Cohen, A. 63n, 68n
colonialism ix, 2ff, 7, 11, 17, 23ff, 27,
    32, 33, 59, 62, 66n, 72, 74ff
commerce 15f, 19
communalism 7f, 58–78
communal strife ix, 8, 35, 59 *et seq*
Conlon, F. 24, 77n
coping with threats 16f, 77
Cornwallis, Lord 23
courts, legal 28f, 32
Crusades 15
culture 10, 34, 65ff

Das Gupta, J. 6
Desai, A. R. 60
Dhanagare, D. N. 60, 63
Dirks, N. B. 6, 47–51
disordered phenomena 7f
Dobbin, C. 24, 29, 59
Dodwell, H. H. 24n
double-entry bookkeeping 16
Dube, S. C. 25n, 59
Duby, G. 12n, 13, 14, 16, 23, 27, 56
Dumont, L. 4n, 5, 21, 30, 33, 34, 60,
    62, 77

Elias, N. 23, 32n
Epstein, T. S. 58
Erasmus 16